Common Worship
Calendar, Lectionary and Collects

Advent 1999 to Advent 2000

Church House Publishing
Church House, Great Smith Street
London SW1P 3NZ

Published 1999 by Church House Publishing

ISBN 0 7151 3825 1

The Archbishops' Council is indebted to the Churches, societies, publishers and individuals whose copyright texts have been included in *Calendar, Lectionary and Collects*, either in original or in adapted form. For details see *Calendar, Lectionary and Collects* Source and Copyright Information and *Acknowledgements* on page 96 of this book.

Authorization
The Calendar, Lectionary, Collects and Post Communions in this publication are authorized pursuant to Canon B 2 of the Canons of the Church of England for use from 30 November 1997 until further resolution of the General Synod of the Church of England.

Editorial, cover and page design by A D Publishing Services.
Printed in England by University Printing House, Cambridge

Common Worship

Calendar, Lectionary and Collects

Advent 1999
to
Advent 2000

Introduction

This book is a compilation of the collects, post communions and lectionary readings for the Sundays and Principal Festivals between Advent 1999 and Advent 2000. It is essentially a version of *The Christian Year: Calendar, Lectionary and Collects*, for the year 2000, providing all that is needed by those preparing services.

The title of the Sunday (or feast day), the date and the colour of the season are indicated at the top of the entry; the season is indicated in the page footer.

Notes on the calendar

Sundays

All Sundays celebrate the paschal mystery of the death and resurrection of the Lord. Nevertheless, they also reflect the character of the seasons in which they are set.

Principal feasts

On these days the Holy Communion is celebrated in every cathedral and parish church, and this celebration, required by Canon B 14, may only be dispensed with in accordance with the provision of Canon B 14 A.

These days, and the liturgical provision for them, may not be displaced by any other celebration.

Except in the case of Christmas Day and Easter Day, **the celebration of the feast begins with Evening Prayer on the day before the feast**, and the collect at that Evening Prayer is that of the feast. In the case of Christmas Eve and Easter Eve, there is proper liturgical provision, including a collect, for the Eve, and this is used at both Morning and Evening Prayer.

The Epiphany is celebrated on Thursday 6 January but may, for pastoral reasons, be celebrated on Sunday 2 January, thus replacing the provision for the Second Sunday of Christmas.

The Presentation of Christ in the Temple (Candlemas) is celebrated either on Wednesday 2 February or on Sunday 30 January, thus replacing the provision for the Fourth Sunday of Epiphany.

All Saints' Day is celebrated on either Wednesday 1 November or Sunday 5 November; if the latter is chosen, there may be a secondary celebration on 1 November.

Other principal holy days

These days, and the liturgical provision for them, may not be displaced by any other celebration.

Ash Wednesday (8 March) and **Maundy Thursday** (20 April) are Principal Holy Days. On both these days the Holy Communion is celebrated in every cathedral or parish church, except where there is dispensation under Canon B 14 A.

Good Friday (21 April) is a Principal Holy Day.

Eastertide

The paschal character of **the Great Fifty Days of Eastertide**, from Easter Day (23 April) to Pentecost (11 June), should be celebrated throughout the season, and should not be displaced by other celebrations. Except for a patronal or dedication festival, no festival may displace the celebration of Sunday as a memorial of the resurrection and no saint's day may be celebrated in Easter Week. The paschal character of the season should be retained on those weekdays when saints' days are celebrated.

Rogation Days are the three days before Ascension Day (29 to 31 May), when prayer is offered for God's blessing on the fruits of the earth and on human labour.

The nine days after Ascension Day until Pentecost (2 to 10 June) are days of prayer and preparation to celebrate the outpouring of the Spirit.

Festivals

These days and the liturgical provision for them are not usually displaced. For each day there is full liturgical provision for the Holy Communion and for Morning and Evening Prayer.

Provision is also made for a first Evening Prayer on the day before the festival where this is required.

Festivals falling on a Sunday may be kept on that day or transferred to the Monday (or, at the discretion of the minister, to the next suitable weekday). But a festival may not be celebrated on Sundays in Advent, Lent or Eastertide. Festivals coinciding with a Principal Feast or a Principal Holy Day are transferred to the first available day.

Mothering Sunday falls on 2 April 2000, the Fourth Sunday of Lent. Alternative prayers and readings are provided for the Principal Service.

The Thursday after Trinity Sunday (22 June 2000) may be observed as the **Day of Thanksgiving for the Holy Communion** (sometimes known as ***Corpus Christi***), and may be kept as a festival.

The festival of **Joseph of Nazareth** is transferred to Monday 20 March 2000.

The festival of **George, Martyr, Patron of England** in 2000 is transferred from 23 April (Easter Day) to Tuesday 2 May.

The festival of **Mark the Evangelist** in 2000 is transferred from 25 April (in Easter Week) to Wednesday 3 May.

The festival of **Matthias the Apostle** falls on Sunday 14 May 1999, the Fourth Sunday of Easter, and is transferred to Monday 15 May.

The festival of **Barnabas the Apostle** falls on the feast of Sunday 11 June 1999, the feast of Pentecost, and is transferred to Monday 12 June.

The festival of **The Transfiguration of our Lord** falls on Sunday 6 August 2000. It displaces the Seventh Sunday after Trinity, unless transferred to Monday 7 August.

Bible Sunday may be celebrated on 29 October, displacing the Last Sunday after Trinity, and appropriate readings are provided.

Local celebrations

The celebration of **the patron saint** or **the title of a church** is kept either as a Festival or as a Principal Feast.

If *either* **George** or **Mark** are patronal festivals and are being observed as principal feasts *either* may be celebrated on Sunday 30 April, displacing the provision for the Second Sunday of Easter.

The **Dedication Festival** of a church is the anniversary of the date of its dedication or consecration. This is kept either as a Festival or as a Principal Feast. When kept as Principal Feasts, the Patronal and Dedication Festivals may be transferred to the nearest Sunday, unless that day is already a Principal Feast or one of the following days: the First Sunday of Advent, the Baptism of Christ, the First Sunday of Lent, the Fifth Sunday of Lent or Palm Sunday. If the date of dedication is unknown, the Dedication Festival may be observed on 1 October (displacing the Fifteenth Sunday after Trinity) or 29 October (displacing the Last Sunday after Trinity). Prayers and readings can be found on page 83.

Harvest Thanksgiving may be celebrated on any Sunday in autumn, replacing the provision for that day, provided it does not supersede any Principal Feast or Festival. The readings are: Deuteronomy 8.8-17 *or* 28.1-14; Psalm 65; 2 Corinthians 9.6-15; Luke 12.16-30 *or* 17.11-19.

In **the calendar of the saints**, diocesan and other local provision may be made to supplement the national calendar.

Lesser festivals

Lesser Festivals, which are listed in the calendar, are observed at the level appropriate to a particular church. Each is provided with a collect, psalm and readings, which may supersede the collect of the week and the daily eucharistic lectionary. The daily psalms and readings at Morning and Evening Prayer are not usually superseded by those for Lesser Festivals, but at the minister's discretion psalms and readings provided on these days for the Holy Communion may be used at Morning and Evening Prayer.

The minister may be selective in the Lesser Festivals that are observed, and may also keep some or all of them as 'Commemorations'.

When a Lesser Festival falls on a Principal Feast or Holy Day or on a Festival, its celebration is normally omitted for that year, but, where there is sufficient reason, it may, at the discretion of the minister, be celebrated on the nearest available day.

Commemorations

Commemorations, which are listed in the calendar, are made by a mention in prayers of intercession and thanksgiving. They are not provided with collect, psalm and readings and do not replace the usual weekday provision at either the Holy Communion or Morning and Evening Prayer.

The Minister may be selective in the Commemorations that are made.

A Commemoration may be observed as a Lesser Festival, with liturgical provision from the common material for holy men and women, only where there is an established celebration in the wider church or where the day has a special local significance. In designating a commemoration as a Lesser Festival, the Minister must remember the need not to lose the spirit of the season, especially of Advent and Lent, by too many celebrations that detract from its character.

Days of discipline and self-denial

The weekdays of Lent and every Friday in the year are days of discipline and self-denial, except all Principal Feasts and Festivals outside Lent and Fridays from Easter Day to Pentecost.

The Eves of Principal Feasts are also appropriately kept as days of discipline and self-denial in preparation for the feast.

Ember Days

Ember Days should be kept, under the Bishop's directions, in the week before an ordination as days of prayer for those to be made deacon or priest.

Ember Days may also be kept even when there is no ordination in the diocese as more general days of prayer for those who serve the Church in its various ministries, both ordained and lay, and for vocations.

Traditionally they have been observed on the Wednesdays, Fridays and Saturdays within the weeks before the Third Sunday of Advent, the Second Sunday of Lent and the Sundays nearest to 29 June and 29 September. References to them are in Footnotes on the pages of the Calendar.

Ordinary Time

Ordinary Time is the period after the Feast of the Presentation of Christ until Shrove Tuesday, and from the day after the Feast of Pentecost until the day before the First Sunday of Advent. During Ordinary Time, there is no seasonal emphasis, except that the period between All Saints' Day and the First Sunday of Advent is observed as a time to celebrate and reflect upon the reign of Christ in earth and heaven.

Liturgical colours

Appropriate liturgical colours are suggested: they are not mandatory and traditional or local use may be followed.

Notes on the Lectionary

The readings are taken from the Church of England's *Common Worship* lectionary which has been adapted from *The Revised Common Lectionary*. The readings for 1999-2000 are from Year B, which offers a semi-continuous reading of Mark's Gospel at the principal Sunday services throughout the year.

1 All Bible **references** are to the *New Revised Standard Version* of the Bible. Those who use other Bible translations should check the verse numbers against the NRSV.

  The references give book, chapter and verse, in that order. Where optional additional verses or psalms are set, the references are placed in square brackets [...]. A simple choice between two alternative readings is indicated by an italicized *or* ... placed between references. For longer psalms, a shorter alternative is sometimes offered, indicated by an italicized *or* within square brackets [*or* ...].

2 Three sets of psalms and readings are provided for each Sunday.

The **Principal Service lectionary** is intended for use at the principal service of the day (whether this service is the Holy Communion or some other authorized form). In most church communities, this is likely to be the mid-morning service, but the minister is free to decide which service time normally constitutes the principal service of the day.

The **Second Service lectionary** is intended for a second main service. In many churches, this lectionary will be the appropriate provision for a Sunday afternoon or evening service. A Gospel reading is always provided so that this lectionary can, if necessary, be used at the Holy Communion.

The **Third Service lectionary**, with shorter readings, is intended where a third set of psalms and readings is needed and is most appropriate for use at an office. A Gospel reading is not always provided, so this lectionary is not suitable for use at the Holy Communion.

3 If only **two readings** are used at the Principal Service and that service is Holy Communion, the second reading must always be the Gospel reading. When the Principal Service lectionary is used at a service other than the Holy Communion, the Gospel reading need not always be chosen.

If there are only two readings at the Principal Service on Ascension Day or Pentecost, the reading from the Acts of the Apostles must always be used.

4 In the **choice of readings** other than the Gospel reading, the minister should ensure that, in any year, a balance is maintained between readings from the Old and New Testaments and that, where a particular biblical book is appointed to be read over several weeks, the choice ensures that this continuity of one book is not lost.

5 Where a reading from the **Apocrypha** is offered, an alternative Old Testament reading is always provided.

6 On the Sundays after Trinity, the Principal Service lectionary provides **alternative Old Testament readings and psalms**. Those in the right-hand column (under the heading 'Related') relate the Old Testament reading and the psalm to the Gospel reading. Those in the left-hand column (under the heading 'Continuous') offer semi-continuous reading of Old Testament texts but allow the Old Testament reading and its complementary psalm to stand independently of the other readings. It is unhelpful to move from week to week from one column to another. One column should be followed for the whole sequence of Sundays after Trinity.

Notes on Collects

1 A † symbol beside the words *Collect* and *Post Communion* indicates that a traditional form of this prayer exists in *The Book of Common Prayer*, and that the traditional form may be used in place of the text provided here.

2 Where a collect ends 'through Jesus Christ ... now and for ever' the minister may use the shorter ending, 'through Jesus Christ or Lord', to which the people respond 'Amen' and omit the longer Trinitarian ending. The longer ending is to be preferred at the Holy Communion.

3 The collect for each Sunday is used on the following weekdays, except where other provision is made.

The Calendar

Typography

In the printing of the Calendar, Principal Feasts and other Principal Holy Days are printed in **BOLD UPPER CASE**; Festivals are printed in **Bold** typeface; other Sundays and Lesser Festivals are printed in ordinary roman typeface, in black. Commemorations are printed in a smaller typeface in *italics*.

November 1999

28	*Sun*	**The First Sunday of Advent**
		YEAR B begins today
29	*Mon*	*Day of Intercession and Thanksgiving for the Missionary Work of the Church*
30	*Tue*	**Andrew the Apostle**

December 1999

1	*Wed*	*Charles de Foucauld, Hermit in the Sahara, 1916*
2	*Thu*	
3	*Fri*	*Francis Xavier, Missionary, Apostle of the Indies, 1552*
4	*Sat*	*John of Damascus, Monk, Teacher of the Faith, c.749*
		Nicholas Ferrar, Deacon, Founder of the Little Gidding Community, 1637
5	*Sun*	**The Second Sunday of Advent**
6	*Mon*	Nicholas, Bishop of Myra, c.326
7	*Tue*	Ambrose, Bishop of Milan, Teacher of the Faith, 397
8	*Wed*	Conception of the Blessed Virgin Mary
9	*Thu*	
10	*Fri*	
11	*Sat*	
12	*Sun*	**The Third Sunday of Advent**
13	*Mon*	Lucy, Martyr at Syracuse, 304
		Samuel Johnson, Moralist, 1784
14	*Tue*	John of the Cross, Poet, Teacher of the Faith, 1591
15	*Wed*	
16	*Thu*	
17	*Fri*	*O Sapientia*
		Eglantine Jebb, Social Reformer, Founder of 'Save The Children', 1928
18	*Sat*	
19	*Sun*	**The Fourth Sunday of Advent**
20	*Mon*	
21	*Tue*	
22	*Wed*	
23	*Thu*	
24	*Fri*	Christmas Eve
25	*Sat*	**CHRISTMAS DAY**
26	*Sun*	**Stephen, Deacon, First Martyr – The First Sunday of Christmas**
27	*Mon*	**John, Apostle and Evangelist**
28	*Tue*	**The Holy Innocents**
29	*Wed*	Thomas Becket, Archbishop of Canterbury, Martyr, 1170
		or **Stephen, Deacon, First Martyr** *(if transferred from 26 December)*
30	*Thu*	
31	*Fri*	*John Wyclif, Reformer, 1384*

Other Dates

Guidance about **Ember Days** can be found on page 7.
Thomas the Apostle may be celebrated on 21 December instead of 3 July.
Thomas Becket may be celebrated on 7 July instead of 29 December.

January 2000

1	*Sat*	**The Naming and Circumcision of Jesus**
2	*Sun*	**The Second Sunday of Christmas** (*or* THE EPIPHANY *if transferred from 6 January*)
3	*Mon*	
4	*Tue*	
5	*Wed*	
6	*Thu*	THE EPIPHANY
7	*Fri*	
8	*Sat*	
9	*Sun*	**The Baptism of Christ** – *The First Sunday of Epiphany*
10	*Mon*	*William Laud, Archbishop of Canterbury, 1645*
11	*Tue*	*Mary Slessor, Missionary in West Africa, 1915*
12	*Wed*	Aelred of Hexham, Abbot of Rievaulx, 1167 *Benedict Biscop, Abbot of Wearmouth, Scholar, 689*
13	*Thu*	Hilary, Bishop of Poitiers, Teacher of the Faith, 367 *Kentigern (Mungo), Missionary Bishop in Strathclyde and Cumbria, 603* *George Fox, Founder of the Society of Friends (the Quakers), 1691*
14	*Fri*	
15	*Sat*	
16	*Sun*	**The Second Sunday of Epiphany**
17	*Mon*	Antony of Egypt, Hermit, Abbot, 356 *Charles Gore, Bishop, Founder of the Community of the Resurrection, 1932*
18-25		*Week of Prayer for Christian Unity*
18	*Tue*	
19	*Wed*	Wulfstan, Bishop of Worcester, 1095
20	*Thu*	*Richard Rolle of Hampole, Spiritual Writer, 1349*
21	*Fri*	Agnes, Child-Martyr at Rome, 304
22	*Sat*	*Vincent of Saragossa, Deacon, First Martyr of Spain, 304*
23	*Sun*	**The Third Sunday of Epiphany**
24	*Mon*	Francis de Sales, Bishop of Geneva, Teacher of the Faith, 1622
25	*Tue*	**The Conversion of Paul**
26	*Wed*	Timothy and Titus, Companions of Paul
27	*Thu*	
28	*Fri*	Thomas Aquinas, Priest, Philosopher, Teacher of the Faith, 1274
29	*Sat*	
30	*Sun*	**The Fourth Sunday of Epiphany** (*or* THE PRESENTATION OF CHRIST IN THE TEMPLE *if transferred from 2 February. If so, Ordinary Time begins on Monday 31 January)*
31	*Mon*	

Lesser Festivals and Commemorations

omitted this year except, where appropriate, by a mention in prayer

2	Basil the Great and Gregory of Nazianzus, Bishops, Teachers of the Faith, 379 and 389
2	*Seraphim, Monk of Sarov, Spiritual Guide, 1833*
2	*Vedanayagam Samuel Azariah, Bishop in South India, Evangelist, 1945*
30	Charles, King and Martyr, 1649
31	*John Bosco, Priest, Founder of the Salesian Teaching Order, 1888*

February 2000

1 *Tue* *Brigid, Abbess of Kildare, c.525*
2 *Wed* THE PRESENTATION OF CHRIST IN THE TEMPLE – CANDLEMAS
3 *Thu* *Ordinary Time begins*
Anskar, Archbishop of Hamburg, Missionary in Denmark and Sweden, 865
4 *Fri* *Gilbert of Sempringham, Founder of the Gilbertine Order, 1189*
5 *Sat*
6 *Sun* **The Fifth Sunday Before Lent**
7 *Mon*
8 *Tue*
9 *Wed*
10 *Thu* *Scholastica, sister of Benedict, Abbess of Plombariola, c.543*
11 *Fri*
12 *Sat*
13 *Sun* **The Fourth Sunday Before Lent**
14 *Mon* Cyril and Methodius, Missionaries to the Slavs, 869 and 885
Valentine, Martyr at Rome, c.269
15 *Tue* *Sigfrid, Bishop, Apostle of Sweden, 1045*
Thomas Bray, Priest, Founder of the SPCK and the SPG, 1730
16 *Wed*
17 *Thu* Janani Luwum, Archbishop of Uganda, Martyr, 1977
18 *Fri*
19 *Sat*
20 *Sun* **The Third Sunday Before Lent**
21 *Mon*
22 *Tue*
23 *Wed* Polycarp, Bishop of Smyrna, Martyr, c.155
24 *Thu*
25 *Fri*
26 *Sat*
27 *Sun* **The Second Sunday Before Lent**
28 *Mon*
29 *Tue*

Lesser Festivals and Commemorations

omitted this year except, where appropriate, by a mention in prayer
6 *The Martyrs of Japan, 1597*
27 George Herbert, Priest, Poet, 1633

Other Dates

The Accession of Queen Elizabeth II may be observed on 6 February.
Matthias may be celebrated on 24 February instead of 14 May.
Guidance about **Ember Days** can be found on page 7.

March 2000

1	*Wed*	David, Bishop of Menevia, Patron of Wales, c.601
2	*Thu*	Chad, Bishop of Lichfield, Missionary, 672
3	*Fri*	
4	*Sat*	
5	*Sun*	**The Sunday Next Before Lent**
6	*Mon*	
7	*Tue*	Perpetua, Felicity and their Companions, Martyrs at Carthage, 203
8	*Wed*	ASH WEDNESDAY
9	*Thu*	
10	*Fri*	
11	*Sat*	
12	*Sun*	**The First Sunday of Lent**
13	*Mon*	
14	*Tue*	
15	*Wed*	
16	*Thu*	
17	*Fri*	Patrick, Bishop, Missionary, Patron of Ireland, c.460
18	*Sat*	*Cyril, Bishop of Jerusalem, Teacher of the Faith, 386*
19	*Sun*	**The Second Sunday of Lent**
20	*Mon*	**Joseph of Nazareth** *(transferred from 19 March)*
21	*Tue*	Thomas Cranmer, Archbishop of Canterbury, Reformation Martyr, 1556
22	*Wed*	
23	*Thu*	
24	*Fri*	*Walter Hilton of Thurgarton, Augustinian Canon, Mystic, 1396* *Oscar Romero, Archbishop of San Salvador, Martyr, 1980*
25	*Sat*	THE ANNUNCIATION OF OUR LORD TO THE BLESSED VIRGIN MARY
26	*Sun*	**The Third Sunday of Lent**
27	*Mon*	
28	*Tue*	
29	*Wed*	
30	*Thu*	
31	*Fri*	*John Donne, Priest, Poet, 1631*

Lesser Festivals and Commemorations

omitted this year except, where appropriate, by a mention in prayer

8 Edward King, Bishop of Lincoln, 1910
8 *Felix, Bishop, Apostle to the East Angles, 647; Geoffrey Studdert Kennedy, Priest, Poet, 1929*
20 Cuthbert, Bishop of Lindisfarne, Missionary, 687
26 *Harriet Monsell, Founder of the Community of St John the Baptist, Clewer, 1883*

Other Dates

Chad may be celebrated with Cedd on 26 October instead of 2 March.
Cuthbert may be celebrated on 4 September instead of 20 March.

April 2000

1	*Sat*	*Frederick Denison Maurice, Priest, Teacher of the Faith, 1872*
2	*Sun*	**The Fourth Sunday of Lent** – *Mothering Sunday*
3	*Mon*	
4	*Tue*	
5	*Wed*	
6	*Thu*	
7	*Fri*	
8	*Sat*	
9	*Sun*	**The Fifth Sunday of Lent** – *Passiontide begins*
10	*Mon*	William Law, Priest, Spiritual Writer, 1761 *William of Ockham, Friar, Philosopher, Teacher of the Faith, 1347*
11	*Tue*	*George Augustus Selwyn, First Bishop of New Zealand, 1878*
12	*Wed*	
13	*Thu*	
14	*Fri*	
15	*Sat*	
16	*Sun*	**Palm Sunday**
17	*Mon*	Monday in Holy Week
18	*Tue*	Tuesday in Holy Week
19	*Wed*	Wednesday in Holy Week
20	*Thu*	**MAUNDY THURSDAY**
21	*Fri*	**GOOD FRIDAY**
22	*Sat*	Easter Eve
23	*Sun*	**EASTER DAY**
24	*Mon*	Monday in Easter Week
25	*Tue*	Tuesday in Easter Week
26	*Wed*	Wednesday in Easter Week
27	*Thu*	Thursday in Easter Week
28	*Fri*	Friday in Easter Week
29	*Sat*	Saturday in Easter Week
30	*Sun*	**The Second Sunday of Easter**

Lesser Festivals and Commemorations

omitted this year except, where appropriate, by a mention in prayer

9	*Dietrich Bonhoeffer, Lutheran Pastor, Martyr, 1945*
16	*Isabella Gilmore, Deaconess, 1923*
19	Alphege, Archbishop of Canterbury, Martyr, 1012
21	Anselm, Abbot of Le Bec, Archbishop of Canterbury, Teacher of the Faith, 1109
24	*Mellitus, Bishop of London, First Bishop at St Paul's, 624*
27	*Christina Rossetti, Poet, 1894*
28	*Peter Chanel, Missionary in the South Pacific, Martyr, 1841*
29	Catherine of Siena, Teacher of the Faith, 1380
30	*Pandita Mary Ramabai, Translator of the Scriptures, 1922*

May 2000

1	*Mon*	**Philip and James, Apostles**
2	*Tue*	**George, Martyr, Patron of England**, c.304 *(transferred from 23 April)*
3	*Wed*	**Mark the Evangelist** *(transferred from 25 April)*
4	*Thu*	English Saints and Martyrs of the Reformation Era
5	*Fri*	
6	*Sat*	
7	*Sun*	**The Third Sunday of Easter**
8	*Mon*	Julian of Norwich, Spiritual Writer, c.1417
9	*Tue*	
10	*Wed*	
11	*Thu*	
12	*Fri*	
13	*Sat*	
14	*Sun*	**The Fourth Sunday of Easter**
15	*Mon*	**Matthias the Apostle** *(transferred from 14 May)*
16	*Tue*	*Caroline Chisholm, Social Reformer, 1877*
17	*Wed*	
18	*Thu*	
19	*Fri*	Dunstan, Archbishop of Canterbury, Restorer of Monastic Life, 988
20	*Sat*	Alcuin of York, Deacon, Abbot of Tours, 804
21	*Sun*	**The Fifth Sunday of Easter**
22	*Mon*	
23	*Tue*	*Petroc, Abbot of Padstow, 6th century*
24	*Wed*	John and Charles Wesley, Evangelists, Hymn Writers, 1791 and 1788
25	*Thu*	The Venerable Bede, Monk at Jarrow, Scholar, Historian, 735 *Aldhelm, Bishop of Sherborne, 709*
26	*Fri*	Augustine, First Archbishop of Canterbury, 605 *John Calvin, Reformer, 1564* *Philip Neri, Founder of the Oratorians, Spiritual Guide, 1595*
27	*Sat*	
28	*Sun*	**The Sixth Sunday of Easter**
29	*Mon*	
30	*Tue*	Josephine Butler, Social Reformer, 1906 *Joan of Arc, Visionary, 1431* *Apolo Kivebulaya, Priest, Evangelist in Central Africa, 1933*
31	*Wed*	**The Visit of the Blessed Virgin Mary to Elizabeth**

Lesser Festivals and Commemorations

omitted this year except, where appropriate, by a mention in prayer

2 Athanasius, Bishop of Alexandria, Teacher of the Faith, 373
21 *Helena, Protector of the Holy Places, 330*
28 *Lanfranc, Prior of Le Bec, Archbishop of Canterbury, Scholar, 1089*

Other Dates

The Visit of the Blessed Virgin Mary to Elizabeth may be celebrated on 2 July instead of 31 May.
Matthias may be celebrated on 24 February instead of 14 May.

June 2000

1	*Thu*	ASCENSION DAY
2	*Fri*	*From Friday after Ascension Day begin the nine days of prayer before Pentecost*
3	*Sat*	*The Martyrs of Uganda, 1886 and 1978*
4	*Sun*	**The Seventh Sunday of Easter** – *Sunday after Ascension Day*
5	*Mon*	Boniface (Wynfrith) of Crediton, Bishop, Apostle of Germany, Martyr, 754
6	*Tue*	*Ini Kopuria, Founder of the Melanesian Brotherhood, 1945*
7	*Wed*	
8	*Thu*	Thomas Ken, Bishop of Bath and Wells, Non-Juror, Hymn Writer, 1711
9	*Fri*	Columba, Abbot of Iona, Missionary, 597 *Ephrem of Syria, Deacon, Hymn Writer, Teacher of the Faith, 373*
10	*Sat*	
11	*Sun*	**PENTECOST (Whit Sunday)**
12	*Mon*	**Barnabas the Apostle** *(transferred from 11 June)*
13	*Tue*	*Ordinary Time resumes*
14	*Wed*	*Richard Baxter, Puritan Divine, 1691*
15	*Thu*	*Evelyn Underhill, Spiritual Writer, 1941*
16	*Fri*	Richard, Bishop of Chichester, 1253 *Joseph Butler, Bishop of Durham, Philosopher, 1752*
17	*Sat*	*Samuel and Henrietta Barnett, Social Reformers, 1913 and 1936*
18	*Sun*	**TRINITY SUNDAY**
19	*Mon*	*Sundar Singh of India, Sadhu (holy man), Evangelist, Teacher of the Faith, 1929*
20	*Tue*	
21	*Wed*	
22	*Thu*	**The Day of Thanksgiving for the Institution of Holy Communion – Corpus Christi** *may be celebrated as a Festival or* Alban, first Martyr of Britain, c.250
23	*Fri*	Etheldreda, Abbess of Ely, c.678
24	*Sat*	**The Birth of John the Baptist**
25	*Sun*	**The First Sunday After Trinity**
26	*Mon*	
27	*Tue*	*Cyril, Bishop of Alexandria, Teacher of the Faith, 444*
28	*Wed*	Irenæus, Bishop of Lyons, Teacher of the Faith, c.200
29	*Thu*	**Peter and Paul, Apostles** *or* **Peter the Apostle**
30	*Fri*	

Lesser Festivals and Commemorations

omitted this year except, where appropriate, by a mention in prayer

1 Justin, Martyr at Rome, c.165
18 *Bernard Mizeki, Apostle of the MaShona, Martyr, 1896*

Other Dates

Guidance about **Ember Days** can be found on page 7.
Peter the Apostle may be celebrated alone, without Paul, on 29 June.

July 2000

1 *Sat* *John and Henry Venn, Priests, Evangelical Divines, 1813 and 1873*
2 *Sun* **The Second Sunday After Trinity**
3 *Mon* **Thomas the Apostle**
4 *Tue*
5 *Wed*
6 *Thu* *Thomas More, Scholar, and John Fisher, Bishop of Rochester, Reformation Martyrs, 1535*
7 *Fri*
8 *Sat*
9 *Sun* **The Third Sunday After Trinity**
10 *Mon*
11 *Tue* Benedict of Nursia, Abbot of Monte Cassino, Father of Western Monasticism, c.550
12 *Wed*
13 *Thu*
14 *Fri* John Keble, Priest, Tractarian, Poet, 1866
15 *Sat* Swithun, Bishop of Winchester, c.862
Bonaventure, Friar, Bishop, Teacher of the Faith, 1274
16 *Sun* **The Fourth Sunday After Trinity**
17 *Mon*
18 *Tue* *Elizabeth Ferard, First Deaconess of the Church of England, 1883*
19 *Wed* Gregory, Bishop of Nyssa, and his sister Macrina, Deaconess, Teachers of the Faith, 394 and 379
20 *Thu* *Margaret of Antioch, Martyr, 4th Century*
Bartolomé de las Casas, Apostle to the Indies, 1566
21 *Fri*
22 *Sat* **Mary Magdalene**
23 *Sun* **The Fifth Sunday After Trinity**
24 *Mon*
25 *Tue* **James the Apostle**
26 *Wed* Anne and Joachim, Parents of the Blessed Virgin Mary
27 *Thu* *Brooke Foss Westcott, Bishop of Durham, Teacher of the Faith, 1901*
28 *Fri*
29 *Sat* Mary, Martha and Lazarus, Companions of our Lord
30 *Sun* **The Sixth Sunday After Trinity**
31 *Mon* *Ignatius of Loyola, Founder of the Society of Jesus, 1556*

Lesser Festivals and Commemorations

omitted this year except, where appropriate, by a mention in prayer
16 *Osmund, Bishop of Salisbury, 1099*
23 *Bridget of Sweden, Abbess of Vadstena, 1373*
30 William Wilberforce, Social Reformer, 1833

Other Dates

The Visit of the Blessed Virgin Mary to Elizabeth may be celebrated on 2 July instead of 31 May.
Thomas the Apostle may be celebrated on 21 December instead of 3 July.
Thomas Becket may be celebrated on 7 July instead of 29 December.

August 2000

1	*Tue*	
2	*Wed*	
3	*Thu*	
4	*Fri*	*Jean-Baptist Vianney,* Curé d'Ars, *Spiritual Guide, 1859*
5	*Sat*	Oswald, King of Northumbria, Martyr, 642
6	*Sun*	**The Transfiguration of our Lord – The Seventh Sunday After Trinity**
7	*Mon*	**The Transfiguration of our Lord** *(if transferred from 6 August)* *John Mason Neale, Priest, Hymn Writer, 1866*
8	*Tue*	Dominic, Priest, Founder of the Order of Preachers, 1221
9	*Wed*	Mary Sumner, Founder of the Mothers' Union, 1921
10	*Thu*	Laurence, Deacon at Rome, Martyr, 258
11	*Fri*	Clare of Assisi, Founder of the Minoresses (Poor Clares), 1253 *John Henry Newman, Priest, Tractarian, 1890*
12	*Sat*	
13	*Sun*	**The Eighth Sunday After Trinity**
14	*Mon*	*Maximilian Kolbe, Friar, Martyr, 1941*
15	*Tue*	**The Blessed Virgin Mary**
16	*Wed*	
17	*Thu*	
18	*Fri*	
19	*Sat*	
20	*Sun*	**The Ninth Sunday After Trinity**
21	*Mon*	
22	*Tue*	
23	*Wed*	
24	*Thu*	**Bartholomew the Apostle**
25	*Fri*	
26	*Sat*	
27	*Sun*	**The Tenth Sunday After Trinity**
28	*Mon*	Augustine, Bishop of Hippo, Teacher of the Faith, 430
29	*Tue*	The Beheading of John the Baptist
30	*Wed*	John Bunyan, Spiritual Writer, 1688
31	*Thu*	Aidan, Bishop of Lindisfarne, Missionary, 651

Lesser Festivals and Commemorations

omitted this year except, where appropriate, by a mention in prayer

13 Jeremy Taylor, Bishop of Down and Connor, Teacher of the Faith, 1667
Florence Nightingale, Nurse, Social Reformer, 1910
Octavia Hill, Social Reformer, 1912

20 Bernard, Abbot of Clairvaux, Teacher of the Faith, 1153
William and Catherine Booth, Founders of the Salvation Army, 1912 and 1890

27 Monica, mother of Augustine of Hippo, 387

Other Dates

The Festival of the Blessed Virgin Mary may be celebrated on 8 September instead of 15 August.

September 2000

1	*Fri*	*Giles of Provence, Hermit, c.710*
2	*Sat*	*The Martyrs of Papua New Guinea, 1901 and 1942*
3	*Sun*	**The Eleventh Sunday After Trinity**
4	*Mon*	*Birinus, Bishop of Dorchester (Oxon), Apostle of Wessex, 650*
5	*Tue*	
6	*Wed*	*Allen Gardiner, Missionary, Founder of the South American Mission Society, 1851*
7	*Thu*	
8	*Fri*	The Birth of the Blessed Virgin Mary
9	*Sat*	*Charles Fuge Lowder, Priest, 1880*
10	*Sun*	**The Twelfth Sunday After Trinity**
11	*Mon*	
12	*Tue*	
13	*Wed*	John Chrysostom, Bishop of Constantinople, Teacher of the Faith, 407
14	*Thu*	**Holy Cross Day**
15	*Fri*	Cyprian, Bishop of Carthage, Martyr, 258
16	*Sat*	Ninian, Bishop of Galloway, Apostle of the Picts, c.432 *Edward Bouverie Pusey, Priest, Tractarian, 1882*
17	*Sun*	**The Thirteenth Sunday After Trinity**
18	*Mon*	
19	*Tue*	*Theodore of Tarsus, Archbishop of Canterbury, 690*
20	*Wed*	John Coleridge Patteson, First Bishop of Melanesia, and his Companions, Martyrs, 1871
21	*Thu*	**Matthew, Apostle and Evangelist**
22	*Fri*	
23	*Sat*	
24	*Sun*	**The Fourteenth Sunday after Trinity**
25	*Mon*	Lancelot Andrewes, Bishop of Winchester, Spiritual Writer, 1626 *Sergei of Radonezh, Russian Monastic Reformer, Teacher of the Faith, 1392*
26	*Tue*	*Wilson Carlile, Founder of the Church Army, 1942*
27	*Wed*	Vincent de Paul, Founder of the Congregation of the Mission (Lazarists), 1660
28	*Thu*	
29	*Fri*	**Michael and All Angels**
30	*Sat*	*Jerome, Translator of the Scriptures, Teacher of the Faith, 420*

Lesser Festivals and Commemorations

omitted this year except, where appropriate, by a mention in prayer

3 Gregory the Great, Bishop of Rome, Teacher of the Faith, 604

17 Hildegard, Abbess of Bingen, Visionary, 1179

Other Dates

Cuthbert may be celebrated on 4 September instead of 20 March.

The Festival of the Blessed Virgin Mary may be celebrated on 8 September instead of 15 August.

Guidance about **Ember Days** can be found on page 7.

October 2000

1	*Sun*	**The Fifteenth Sunday After Trinity** *(or* **Feast of Dedication***)*
2	*Mon*	
3	*Tue*	
4	*Wed*	Francis of Assisi, Friar, Deacon, Founder of the Friars Minor, 1226
5	*Thu*	
6	*Fri*	William Tyndale, Translator of the Scriptures, Reformation Martyr, 1536
7	*Sat*	
8	*Sun*	**The Sixteenth Sunday After Trinity**
9	*Mon*	*Denys, Bishop of Paris, and his Companions, Martyrs, c.250* *Robert Grosseteste, Bishop of Lincoln, Philosopher, Scientist, 1253*
10	*Tue*	Paulinus, Bishop of York, Missionary, 644 *Thomas Traherne, Poet, Spiritual Writer, 1674*
11	*Wed*	*Ethelburga, Abbess of Barking, 675* *James the Deacon, companion of Paulinus, 7th century*
12	*Thu*	Wilfrid of Ripon, Bishop, Missionary, 709 *Elizabeth Fry, Prison Reformer, 1845* *Edith Cavell, Nurse, 1915*
13	*Fri*	Edward the Confessor, King of England, 1066
14	*Sat*	
15	*Sun*	**The Seventeenth Sunday After Trinity**
16	*Mon*	*Nicholas Ridley, Bishop of London, and Hugh Latimer, Bishop of Worcester, Reformation Martyrs, 1555*
17	*Tue*	Ignatius, Bishop of Antioch, Martyr, c.107
18	*Wed*	**Luke the Evangelist**
19	*Thu*	Henry Martyn, Translator of the Scriptures, Missionary, 1812
20	*Fri*	
21	*Sat*	
22	*Sun*	**The Eighteenth Sunday After Trinity**
23	*Mon*	
24	*Tue*	
25	*Wed*	*Crispin and Crispinian, Martyrs at Rome, c.287*
26	*Thu*	Alfred the Great, King of the West Saxons, Scholar, 899 *Cedd, Abbot of Lastingham, Bishop of the East Saxons, 664*
27	*Fri*	
28	*Sat*	**Simon and Jude, Apostles**
29	*Sun*	**The Last Sunday After Trinity** – *Bible Sunday*
30	*Mon*	
31	*Tue*	*Martin Luther, Reformer, 1546*

Lesser Festivals and Commemorations

omitted this year except, where appropriate, by a mention in prayer

1	*Remigius, Bishop of Rheims, Apostle of the Franks, 533* *Anthony Ashley Cooper, Earl of Shaftesbury, Social Reformer, 1885*
15	Teresa of Avila, Teacher of the Faith, 1582
29	James Hannington, Bishop, Martyr in Uganda, 1885

Other Dates

Chad may be celebrated with Cedd on 26 October instead of 2 March.

November 2000

1 *Wed* ALL SAINTS' DAY
2 *Thu* Commemoration of the Faithful Departed (All Souls' Day)
3 *Fri* Richard Hooker, Priest, Anglican Apologist, Teacher of the Faith, 1600
Martin de Porres, Friar, 1639
4 *Sat*
5 *Sun* **The Fourth Sunday Before Advent** – *All Saints' Sunday* (*or* ALL SAINTS' DAY *if transferred from 1 November)*
6 *Mon* *Leonard, Hermit, 6th century*
William Temple, Archbishop of Canterbury, Teacher of the Faith, 1944
7 *Tue* Willibrord of York, Bishop, Apostle of Frisia, 739
8 *Wed* The Saints and Martyrs of England
9 *Thu* *Margery Kempe, Mystic, c.1440*
10 *Fri* Leo the Great, Bishop of Rome, Teacher of the Faith, 461
11 *Sat* Martin, Bishop of Tours, c.397
12 *Sun* **The Third Sunday Before Advent** – *Remembrance Sunday*
13 *Mon* Charles Simeon, Priest, Evangelical Divine, 1836
14 *Tue* *Samuel Seabury, First Anglican Bishop in North America, 1796*
15 *Wed*
16 *Thu* Margaret, Queen of Scotland, Philanthropist, Reformer of the Church, 1093
Edmund Rich of Abingdon, Archbishop of Canterbury, 1240
17 *Fri* Hugh, Bishop of Lincoln, 1200
18 *Sat* Elizabeth of Hungary, Princess of Thuringia, Philanthropist, 1231
19 *Sun* **The Second Sunday Before Advent**
20 *Mon* Edmund, King of the East Angles, Martyr, 870
Priscilla Lydia Sellon, a Restorer of the Religious Life in the Church of England, 1876
21 *Tue*
22 *Wed* *Cecilia, Martyr at Rome, c.230*
23 *Thu* Clement, Bishop of Rome, Martyr, c.100
24 *Fri*
25 *Sat* *Catherine of Alexandria, Martyr, 4th century*
Isaac Watts, Hymn Writer, 1748
26 *Sun* **Christ the King** – *The Sunday Next Before Advent*
27 *Mon*
28 *Tue*
29 *Wed* *Day of Intercession and Thanksgiving for the Missionary Work of the Church*
30 *Thu* **Andrew the Apostle**

Lesser Festivals and Commemorations

omitted this year except, where appropriate, by a mention in prayer
19 Hilda, Abbess of Whitby, 680
Mechtild, Béguine of Magdeburg, Mystic, 1280

December 2000

1	*Fri*	*Charles de Foucauld, Hermit in the Sahara, 1916*
2	*Sat*	
3	*Sun*	**The First Sunday of Advent** – *YEAR C begins today*
4	*Mon*	*John of Damascus, Monk, Teacher of the Faith, c.749* *Nicholas Ferrar, Deacon, Founder of the Little Gidding Community, 1637*
5	*Tue*	
6	*Wed*	Nicholas, Bishop of Myra, c.326
7	*Thu*	Ambrose, Bishop of Milan, Teacher of the Faith, 397
8	*Fri*	Conception of the Blessed Virgin Mary
9	*Sat*	
10	*Sun*	**The Second Sunday of Advent**
11	*Mon*	
12	*Tue*	
13	*Wed*	Lucy, Martyr at Syracuse, 304 *Samuel Johnson, Moralist, 1784*
14	*Thu*	John of the Cross, Poet, Teacher of the Faith, 1591
15	*Fri*	
16	*Sat*	
17	*Sun*	**The Third Sunday of Advent** – *O Sapientia*
18	*Mon*	
19	*Tue*	
20	*Wed*	
21	*Thu*	
22	*Fri*	
23	*Sat*	
24	*Sun*	**The Fourth Sunday of Advent** – *Christmas Eve*
25	*Mon*	**CHRISTMAS DAY**
26	*Tue*	**Stephen, Deacon, First Martyr**
27	*Wed*	**John, Apostle and Evangelist**
28	*Thu*	**The Holy Innocents**
29	*Fri*	Thomas Becket, Archbishop of Canterbury, Martyr, 1170
30	*Sat*	
31	*Sun*	**The First Sunday of Christmas**

Lesser Festivals and Commemorations

omitted this year except, where appropriate, by a mention in prayer

3	*Francis Xavier, Missionary, Apostle of the Indies, 1552*
17	*Eglantine Jebb, Social Reformer, Founder of 'Save The Children', 1928*
31	*John Wyclif, Reformer, 1384*

Alternative Dates

Guidance about **Ember Days** can be found on page 7.
Thomas the Apostle may be celebrated on 21 December instead of 3 July.
Thomas Becket may be celebrated on 7 July instead of 29 December.

The First Sunday of Advent

28 November 1999 *Purple*

Collect[†]

Almighty God,
give us grace to cast away the works of darkness
and to put on the armour of light,
now in the time of this mortal life,
in which your Son Jesus Christ
came to us in great humility;
that on the last day,
when he shall come again in his glorious majesty
to judge the living and the dead,
we may rise to the life immortal;
through him who is alive and reigns with you,
in the unity of the Holy Spirit,
one God, now and for ever.

This Collect may be used as the Post Communion on any day of Advent until Christmas Eve instead of the Post Communion provided.

Post Communion

O Lord our God,
make us watchful and keep us faithful
as we await the coming of your Son our Lord;
that, when he shall appear,
he may not find us sleeping in sin
but active in his service
and joyful in his praise;
through Jesus Christ our Lord.

Year B begins today

Principal Service
Isaiah 64.1-9
Psalm 80.1-7 [17-19]
1 Corinthians 1.3-9
Mark 13.24-37

Second Service
Psalm 25 *or* 25.1-10
Isaiah 1.1-20
Matthew 21.1-13

Third Service
Psalm 44
Isaiah 2.1-5
Luke 12.35-48

The Second Sunday of Advent

5 December 1999 ***Purple***

Collect[†]

O Lord, raise up, we pray, your power
and come among us,
and with great might succour us;
that whereas, through our sins and wickedness
we are grievously hindered
in running the race that is set before us,
your bountiful grace and mercy
may speedily help and deliver us;
through Jesus Christ your Son our Lord,
to whom with you and the Holy Spirit,
be honour and glory, now and for ever.

Post Communion

Father in heaven,
who sent your Son to redeem the world
and will send him again to be our judge:
give us grace so to imitate him
in the humility and purity of his first coming
that, when he comes again,
we may be ready to greet him
with joyful love and firm faith;
through Jesus Christ our Lord.

Principal Service
Isaiah 40.1-11
Psalm 85. [1-2] 8-13
2 Peter 3.8-15a
Mark 1.1-8

Second Service
Psalm 40 *or* 40.11-17
1 Kings 22.1-28
Romans 15.4-13
If the Second Service is a Eucharist,
the following is read as a Gospel:
Matthew 11.2-11

Third Service
Psalm 80
Baruch 5.1-9 *or* Zephaniah 3.14-20
Luke 1.5-20

The Third Sunday of Advent

12 December 1999 *Purple*

Collect[†]

O Lord Jesus Christ,
who at your first coming sent your messenger
to prepare your way before you:
grant that the ministers and stewards of your mysteries
may likewise so prepare and make ready your way
by turning the hearts of the disobedient
 to the wisdom of the just,
that at your second coming to judge the world
we may be found an acceptable people in your sight;
for you are alive and reign with the Father
in the unity of the Holy Spirit,
one God, now and for ever.

Post Communion

We give you thanks, O Lord, for these heavenly gifts;
kindle in us the fire of your Spirit
that when your Christ comes again
we may shine as lights before his face;
who is alive and reigns now and for ever.

Principal Service
Isaiah 61.1-4,8-11
Psalm 126 *or Canticle:* Magnificat
1 Thessalonians 5.16-24
John 1.6-8,19-28

Second Service
Psalm 68.1-20 *or* 1-8
Malachi 3.1-4; 4
Philippians 4.4-7
If the Second Service is a Eucharist, the following is read as a Gospel:
Matthew 14.1-12

Third Service
Psalms 50.1-6; 62
Isaiah 12
Luke 1.57-66

The Fourth Sunday of Advent

19 December 1999 *Purple*

Collect

God our redeemer,
who prepared the Blessed Virgin Mary
to be the mother of your Son:
grant that, as she looked for his coming as our saviour,
so we may be ready to greet him
when he comes again as our judge;
who is alive and reigns with you,
in the unity of the Holy Spirit,
one God, now and for ever.

Post Communion

Heavenly Father,
who chose the Blessed Virgin Mary
to be the mother of the promised saviour:
fill us your servants with your grace,
that in all things we may embrace your holy will
and with her rejoice in your salvation;
through Jesus Christ our Lord.

Principal Service
2 Samuel 7.1-11,16
Canticle: Magnificat *or* Psalm 89.1-4,19-26 *or* 89.1-8
Romans 16.25-27
Luke 1.26-38

Second Service
Psalms 113 [131]
Zechariah 2.10-13
Luke 1.39-55

Third Service
Psalm 144
Isaiah 7.10-16
Romans 1.1-7

Christmas Eve

Friday 24 December 1999 *Purple*

Collect

Almighty God,
you make us glad with the yearly remembrance
of the birth of your Son Jesus Christ:
grant that, as we joyfully receive him as our redeemer,
so we may with sure confidence behold him
when he shall come to be our judge;
who is alive and reigns with you,
in the unity of the Holy Spirit,
one God, now and for ever.

Post Communion

Eternal God, for whom we wait,
you have fed us with the bread of eternal life:
keep us ever watchful,
that we may be ready to stand before the Son of Man,
Jesus Christ our Lord.

Morning Eucharist	Evening Prayer
2 Samuel 7.1-5,8-11,16	Psalm 85
Psalm 89.2,21-27	Zechariah 2
Acts 13.16-26	Revelation 1.1-8
Luke 1.67-79	

Christmas Night

Friday 24 / Saturday 25 December 1999 *Gold or White*

Collect

Eternal God,
who made this most holy night
to shine with the brightness of your one true light:
bring us, who have known the revelation
of that light on earth,
to see the radiance of your heavenly glory;
through Jesus Christ your Son our Lord,
who is alive and reigns with you,
in the unity of the Holy Spirit,
one God, now and for ever.

Post Communion

God our Father,
in this night you have made known to us again
the coming of our Lord Jesus Christ:
confirm our faith and fix our eyes on him
until the day dawns
and Christ the Morning Star rises in our hearts.
To him be glory both now and for ever.

Christmas Day

Saturday 25 December 1999 *Gold or White*

Collect[†]

Almighty God,
you have given us your only-begotten Son
to take our nature upon him
and as at this time to be born of a pure virgin:
grant that we, who have been born again
and made your children by adoption and grace,
may daily be renewed by your Holy Spirit;
through Jesus Christ your Son our Lord,
who is alive and reigns with you,
in the unity of the Holy Spirit,
one God, now and for ever.

Post Communion

God our Father,
whose Word has come among us
in the Holy Child of Bethlehem:
may the light of faith illumine our hearts
  and shine in our words and deeds;
through him who is Christ the Lord.

CHRISTMAS DAY Principal Service

Any of these sets of readings may be used on the evening of Christmas Eve and on Christmas Day. Set III should be used at some service during the celebration.

I	II	III
Isaiah 9.2-7	Isaiah 62.6-12	Isaiah 52.7-10
Psalm 96	Psalm 97	Psalm 98
Titus 2.11-14	Titus 3.4-7	Hebrews 1.1-4[5-12]
Luke 2.1-14[15-20]	Luke 2.[1-7]8-20	John 1.1-14

Second Service
Psalm 8
Isaiah 65.17-25
Philippians 2.5-11
or Luke 2.1-20 if it has not been used at the Principal Service of the day

Third Service
Psalm 110
Isaiah 62.1-5
Matthew 1.18-25

Stephen, Deacon, First Martyr

Sunday 26 December 1999 *Red*

Collect

Gracious Father,
who gave the first martyr Stephen
grace to pray for those who took up stones against him:
grant that in all our sufferings for the truth
we may learn to love even our enemies
and to seek forgiveness for those who desire our hurt,
looking up to heaven to him who was crucified for us,
Jesus Christ, our Mediator and Advocate,
who is alive and reigns with you,
in the unity of the Holy Spirit,
one God, now and for ever.

Post Communion

Merciful Lord,
we thank you for the signs of your mercy
revealed in birth and death:
save us by the coming of your Son,
and give us joy in honouring Stephen,
first martyr of the new Israel;
through Jesus Christ our Lord.

St Stephen's Day is celebrated on Sunday 26 December, unless transferred to Wednesday 29 December.

Eucharist

2 Chronicles 24.20-22	*or*	Acts 7.51-60
Psalm 119.161-168		Psalm 119.161-168
Acts 7.51-60		Galatians 2.16b-20
Matthew 23.34-39		Matthew 23.34-39

Morning Prayer
Psalms 13; 31.1-8
Jeremiah 26.12-15
Acts 6

Evening Prayer
Psalms 57, 86
Genesis 4.1-10
Matthew 10.17-22

The First Sunday of Christmas

26 December 1999 *White*

Collect

Almighty God,
who wonderfully created us in your own image
and yet more wonderfully restored us
through your Son Jesus Christ:
grant that, as he came to share in our humanity,
so we may share the life of his divinity;
who is alive and reigns with you,
in the unity of the Holy Spirit,
one God, now and for ever.

Post Communion

Heavenly Father,
whose blessed Son shared at Nazareth
  the life of an earthly home:
help your Church to live as one family,
united in love and obedience,
and bring us all at last to our home in heaven;
through Jesus Christ our Lord.

This provision is used on 26 December only if St Stephen's Day is transferred to Wednesday 29 December.

Principal Service
Isaiah 61.10 – 62.3
Psalm 148 *or* 148.7-14
Galatians 4.4-7
Luke 2.15-21

Second Service
Psalm 132
Isaiah 35.1-10
Colossians 1.9-20 *or* Luke 2.41-52

Third Service
Psalm 105.1-9
Isaiah 63.7-9
Ephesians 3.5-12

The Second Sunday of Christmas

2 January 2000 ***White***

Collect

Almighty God,
in the birth of your Son
you have poured on us the new light of your incarnate Word,
and shown us the fullness of your love:
help us to walk in his light and dwell in his love
that we may know the fullness of his joy;
who is alive and reigns with you,
in the unity of the Holy Spirit,
one God, now and for ever.

Post Communion

All praise to you,
almighty God and heavenly King,
who sent your Son into the world
to take our nature upon him
and to be born of a pure virgin:
grant that, as we are born again in him,
so he may continually dwell in us
and reign on earth as he reigns in heaven,
now and for ever.

The Epiphany may be celebrated on Sunday 2 January in preference to Thursday 6 January, thus replacing the Second Sunday of Christmas.

Principal Service

Jeremiah 31.7-14 *or* Ecclesiasticus 24.1-12
Psalm 147.12-20 *Canticle:* Wisdom of Solomon 10.15-21
Ephesians 1.3-14
John 1.[1-9]10-18

Second Service

Psalm 135 *or* 135.1-14
Isaiah 46.3-13
Romans 12.1-8
If the Second Service is a Eucharist, the following is read as a Gospel:
Matthew 2.13-23

Third Service

Psalm 87
Zechariah 8.1-8
Luke 2.41-52

The Epiphany

Thursday 6 January 2000 ***Gold or White***

Collect[†]

O God,
who by the leading of a star
manifested your only Son to the peoples of the earth:
mercifully grant that we,
who know you now by faith,
may at last behold your glory face to face;
through Jesus Christ your Son our Lord,
who is alive and reigns with you,
in the unity of the Holy Spirit,
one God, now and for ever.

Post Communion

Lord God,
the bright splendour whom the nations seek:
may we who with the wise men
  have been drawn by your light
discern the glory of your presence in your Son,
the Word made flesh, Jesus Christ our Lord.

The Epiphany may be celebrated on Sunday 2 January in preference to Thursday 6 January, thus replacing the Second Sunday of Christmas.
*The liturgical colour is **White** during Epiphany.*

Evening Prayer on the Eve (5 January)
Psalms 96, 97
Isaiah 49.1-13
John 4.7-26

Principal Service
Isaiah 60.1-6
Psalm 72. [1-9]10-15
Ephesians 3.1-12
Matthew 2.1-12

Second Service
Psalms 98, 100
Baruch 4.36 – 5.9 *or* Isaiah 60.1-9
John 2.1-11

Third Service
Psalms 113, 132
Jeremiah 31.7-14
John 1.29-34

The Baptism of Christ

The First Sunday of Epiphany

9 January 2000 *Gold or White*

Collect

Eternal Father,
who at the baptism of Jesus
revealed him to be your Son,
anointing him with the Holy Spirit:
grant to us, who are born again by water and the Spirit,
that we may be faithful to our calling
  as your adopted children;
through Jesus Christ your Son our Lord,
who is alive and reigns with you,
in the unity of the Holy Spirit,
one God, now and for ever.

Post Communion

Lord of all time and eternity,
you opened the heavens
  and revealed yourself as Father
in the baptism of Jesus your beloved Son:
by the power of your Spirit
complete the heavenly work of our rebirth
through the waters of the new creation;
through Jesus Christ our Lord.

This Collect and Post Communion are used throughout the week following.

Evening Prayer on the Eve, if required (8 January)
Psalm 36
Isaiah 61
Titus 2.11-14; 3.4-7

Principal Service
Genesis 1.1-5
Psalm 29
Acts 19.1-7
Mark 1.4-11

Second Service
Psalms 46 [47]
Isaiah 42.1-9
Ephesians 2.1-10
If the Second Service is a Eucharist, the following is read as a Gospel:
Matthew 3.13-17

Third Service
Psalm 89.20-29
1 Samuel 16.1-3,13
John 1.29-34

The Second Sunday of Epiphany

16 January 2000 *White*

Collect

Almighty God,
in Christ you make all things new:
transform the poverty of our nature
  by the riches of your grace,
and in the renewal of our lives
make known your heavenly glory;
through Jesus Christ your Son our Lord,
who is alive and reigns with you,
in the unity of the Holy Spirit,
one God, now and for ever.

Post Communion

God of glory,
you nourish us with your Word
who is the bread of life:
fill us with your Holy Spirit
that through us the light of your glory
may shine in all the world.
We ask this in the name of Jesus Christ our Lord.

Principal Service
1 Samuel 3.1-10[11-20]
Psalm 139.1-6,13-18 *or* 139.1-10
Revelation 5.1-10
John 1.43-51

Second Service
Psalm 96
Isaiah 60.9-22
Hebrews 6.17 – 7.10
If the Second Service is a Eucharist, the following is read as a Gospel:
Matthew 8.5-13

Third Service
Psalm 145.1-12
Isaiah 62.1-5
1 Corinthians 6.11-20

The Third Sunday of Epiphany

23 January 2000 *White*

Collect

Almighty God,
whose Son revealed in signs and miracles
the wonder of your saving presence:
renew your people with your heavenly grace,
and in all our weakness
sustain us by your mighty power;
through Jesus Christ your Son our Lord,
who is alive and reigns with you,
in the unity of the Holy Spirit,
one God, now and for ever.

Post Communion

Almighty Father,
whose Son our Saviour Jesus Christ
  is the light of the world:
may your people,
illumined by your word and sacraments,
shine with the radiance of his glory,
that he may be known, worshipped, and obeyed
  to the ends of the earth;
for he is alive and reigns, now and for ever.

Principal Service
Genesis 14.17-20
Psalm 128
Revelation 19.6-10
John 2.1-11

Second Service
Psalm 33 *or* 33.1-12
Jeremiah 3.21 – 4.2
Titus 2.1-8,11-14
If the Second Service is a Eucharist, the following is read as a Gospel:
Matthew 4.12-23

Third Service
Psalm 113
Jonah 3.1-5,10
John 3.16-21

The Fourth Sunday of Epiphany

30 January 2000 *White*

Collect

God our creator,
who in the beginning
commanded the light to shine out of darkness:
we pray that the light of the glorious gospel of Christ
may dispel the darkness of ignorance and unbelief,
shine into the hearts of all your people,
and reveal the knowledge of your glory
in the face of Jesus Christ your Son our Lord,
who is alive and reigns with you,
in the unity of the Holy Spirit,
one God, now and for ever.

Post Communion

Generous Lord,
in word and eucharist we have proclaimed
the mystery of your love:
help us so to live out our days
that we may be signs of your wonders in the world;
through Jesus Christ our Saviour.

Candlemas (see page 36) may be celebrated on Sunday 30 January, in preference to Wednesday 2 February, thus replacing the Fourth Sunday of Epiphany.

Principal Service
Deuteronomy 18.15-20
Psalm 111
Revelation 12.1-5a
Mark 1.21-28

Second Service
Psalm 34 *or* 34.1-10
1 Samuel 3.1-20
1 Corinthians 14.12-20
If the Second Service is a Eucharist, the following is read as a Gospel:
Matthew 13.10-17

Third Service
Psalm 71.1-6,15-17
Jeremiah 1.4-10
Mark 1.40-45

The Presentation of Christ in the Temple

Candlemas

Wednesday 2 February 2000 *Gold or White*

Collect†

Almighty and ever-living God,
clothed in majesty,
whose beloved Son
was this day presented in the Temple,
in substance of our flesh:
grant that we may be presented to you
with pure and clean hearts,
by your Son Jesus Christ our Lord,
who is alive and reigns with you,
in the unity of the Holy Spirit,
one God, now and for ever.

Post Communion

Lord, you fulfilled the hope of Simeon and Anna,
who lived to welcome the Messiah:
may we, who have received these gifts beyond words,
prepare to meet Christ Jesus when he comes
to bring us to eternal life;
for he is alive and reigns, now and for ever.

Candlemas may be celebrated on Sunday 30 January, in preference to Wednesday 2 February, thus replacing the Fourth Sunday of Epiphany.

Evening Prayer on the Eve (1 February)
Psalm 118
1 Samuel 1.19b-28
Hebrews 4.11-16

Principal Service
Malachi 3.1-5
Psalm 24.[1-6]7-10
Hebrews 2.14-18
Luke 2.22-40

Second Service
Psalms 122, 132
Haggai 2.1-9
John 2.18-22

Third Service
Psalms 42, 43, 48
Exodus 13.1-16
Romans 12.1-5

The Weekdays after Candlemas

Thursday to Saturday, 3 to 5 February 2000 ***Green***

Monday to Saturday, 31 January to 5 February, if Candlemas is celebrated on 30 January.

Collect

Almighty God,
by whose grace alone we are accepted
  and called to your service:
strengthen us by your Holy Spirit
and make us worthy of our calling;
through Jesus Christ your Son our Lord,
who is alive and reigns with you,
in the unity of the Holy Spirit,
one God, now and for ever.

Post Communion

God of truth,
we have seen with our eyes
  and touched with our hands the bread of life:
strengthen our faith
that we may grow in love for you and for each other;
through Jesus Christ our Lord.

The liturgical colour is ***Green*** *from the day after the celebration of Candlemas until Shrove Tuesday (7 March), the day before Ash Wednesday, except where other provision is made.*

The Fifth Sunday Before Lent

6 February 2000 *Green*

Collect

Almighty God,
by whose grace alone we are accepted
and called to your service:
strengthen us by your Holy Spirit
and make us worthy of our calling;
through Jesus Christ your Son our Lord,
who is alive and reigns with you,
in the unity of the Holy Spirit,
one God, now and for ever.

Post Communion

God of truth,
we have seen with our eyes
and touched with our hands the bread of life:
strengthen our faith
that we may grow in love for you and for each other;
through Jesus Christ our Lord.

PROPER 1

Principal Service
Isaiah 40.21-31
Psalm 147,1-11[20c]
1 Corinthians 9.16-23
Mark 1.29-39

Second Service
Psalm 5
Numbers 13.1-2,27-33
Philippians 2.12-28
If the Second Service is a Eucharist, the following is read as a Gospel:
Luke 5.1-11

Third Service
Psalms 2, 3
Jeremiah 26.1-16
Acts 3.1-10

The Fourth Sunday Before Lent

13 February 2000 *Green*

Collect[†]

O God,
you know us to be set
in the midst of so many and great dangers,
that by reason of the frailty of our nature
we cannot always stand upright:
grant to us such strength and protection
as may support us in all dangers
and carry us through all temptations;
through Jesus Christ your Son our Lord,
who is alive and reigns with you,
in the unity of the Holy Spirit,
one God, now and for ever.

Post Communion

Go before us, Lord, in all we do
with your most gracious favour,
and guide us with your continual help,
that in all our works
begun, continued and ended in you,
we may glorify your holy name,
and finally by your mercy receive everlasting life;
through Jesus Christ our Lord.

PROPER 2

Principal Service
2 Kings 5.1-14
Psalm 30
1 Corinthians 9.24-27
Mark 1.40-45

Second Service
Psalm 6
Numbers 20.2-13
Philippians 3.7-21
If the Second Service is a Eucharist, the following is read as a Gospel:
Luke 6.17-26

Third Service
Psalm 7
Jeremiah 30.1-3,10-22
Acts 6

The Third Sunday Before Lent

20 February 2000 *Green*

Collect[†]

Almighty God,
who alone can bring order
to the unruly wills and passions of sinful humanity:
give your people grace
so to love what you command
and to desire what you promise,
that, among the many changes of this world,
our hearts may surely there be fixed
where true joys are to be found;
through Jesus Christ your Son our Lord,
who is alive and reigns with you,
in the unity of the Holy Spirit,
one God, now and for ever.

Post Communion

Merciful Father,
who gave Jesus Christ to be for us the bread of life,
that those who come to him should never hunger:
draw us to the Lord in faith and love,
that we may eat and drink with him
at his table in the kingdom,
where he is alive and reigns, now and for ever.

PROPER 3

Principal Service
Isaiah 43.18-25
Psalm 41
2 Corinthians 1.18-22
Mark 2.1-12

Second Service
Psalm 10
Numbers 22.21 – 23.12
Philippians 4.10-20
If the Second Service is a Eucharist,
the following is read as a Gospel:
Luke 6.27-38

Third Service
Psalm 9
Jeremiah 33.1-11
Acts 8.4-25

The Second Sunday Before Lent

27 February 2000 *Green*

Collect

Almighty God,
you have created the heavens and the earth
and made us in your own image:
teach us to discern your hand in all your works
and your likeness in all your children;
through Jesus Christ your Son our Lord,
who with you and the Holy Spirit
reigns supreme over all things,
now and for ever.

Post Communion

God our creator,
by your gift
the tree of life was set at the heart of the earthly paradise,
and the bread of life at the heart of your Church:
may we who have been nourished at your table on earth
be transformed by the glory of the Saviour's cross
and enjoy the delights of eternity;
through Jesus Christ our Lord.

Principal Service
Proverbs 8.1,22-31
Psalm 104.24-35
Colossians 1.15-20
John 1.1-14

Second Service
Psalm 65
Genesis 2.4b-25
Luke 8.22-35

Third Service
Psalms 29, 67
Deuteronomy 8.1-10
Matthew 6.25-34

The Sunday Next Before Lent

5 March 2000 *Green*

Collect

Almighty Father,
whose Son was revealed in majesty
before he suffered death upon the cross:
give us grace to perceive his glory,
that we may be strengthened to suffer with him
and be changed into his likeness, from glory to glory;
who is alive and reigns with you,
in the unity of the Holy Spirit,
one God, now and for ever.

Post Communion

Holy God,
we see your glory in the face of Jesus Christ:
may we who are partakers at his table
reflect his life in word and deed,
that all the world may know
his power to change and save.
This we ask through Jesus Christ our Lord.

Principal Service
2 Kings 2.1-12
Psalm 50.1-6
2 Corinthians 4.3-6
Mark 9.2-9

Second Service
Psalms 2 [99]
1 Kings 19.1-16
2 Peter 1.16-21
If the Second Service is a Eucharist, the following is read as a Gospel:
Mark 9.[2-8]9-13

Third Service
Psalms 27, 150
Exodus 24.12-18
2 Corinthians 3.12-18

Ash Wednesday

8 March 2000 *Purple or Lent Array*

Collect[†]

Almighty and everlasting God,
you hate nothing that you have made
and forgive the sins of all those who are penitent:
create and make in us new and contrite hearts
that we, worthily lamenting our sins
and acknowledging our wretchedness,
may receive from you, the God of all mercy,
perfect remission and forgiveness;
through Jesus Christ your Son our Lord,
who is alive and reigns with you,
in the unity of the Holy Spirit,
one God, now and for ever.

This Collect may be used as the Post Communion on any day from the First Sunday of Lent until the Saturday after the Fourth Sunday of Lent instead of the Post Communion provided.

Post Communion[†]

Almighty God,
you have given your only Son to be for us
both a sacrifice for sin
and also an example of godly life:
give us grace
that we may always most thankfully receive
these his inestimable gifts,
and also daily endeavour to follow
the blessed steps of his most holy life;
through Jesus Christ our Lord.

Principal Service
Joel 2.1-2,12-17 *or* Isaiah 58.1-12
Psalm 51.1-17
2 Corinthians 5.20b – 6.10
Matthew 6.1-6,16-21 *or* John 8.1-11

Second Service
Psalm 102 *or* 102.1-17
Isaiah 1.10-18
Luke 15.11-32

Third Service
Psalm 38
Daniel 9.3-6,17-19
1 Timothy 6.6-19

The First Sunday of Lent

12 March 2000 *Purple or Lent Array*

Collect

Almighty God,
whose Son Jesus Christ fasted forty days in the wilderness,
and was tempted as we are, yet without sin:
give us grace to discipline ourselves
  in obedience to your Spirit;
and, as you know our weakness,
so may we know your power to save;
through Jesus Christ your Son our Lord,
who is alive and reigns with you,
in the unity of the Holy Spirit,
one God, now and for ever.

Post Communion

Lord God,
you have renewed us with the living bread from heaven;
by it you nourish our faith,
increase our hope,
and strengthen our love:
teach us always to hunger for him
  who is the true and living bread,
and enable us to live by every word
  that proceeds from out of your mouth;
through Jesus Christ our Lord.

Principal Service
Genesis 9.8-17
Psalm 25.1-10
1 Peter 3.18-22
Mark 1.9-15

Second Service
Psalm 119.17-32
Genesis 2.15-17; 3.1-7
Romans 5.12-19 *or* Luke 13.31-35

Third Service
Psalm 77
Exodus 34.1-10
Romans 10.8b-13

The Second Sunday of Lent

19 March 2000 *Purple or Lent Array*

Collect†

Almighty God,
you show to those who are in error the light of your truth,
that they may return to the way of righteousness:
grant to all those who are admitted
  into the fellowship of Christ's religion,
that they may reject those things
  that are contrary to their profession,
and follow all such things as are agreeable to the same;
through our Lord Jesus Christ,
who is alive and reigns with you,
in the unity of the Holy Spirit,
one God, now and for ever.

Post Communion†

Almighty God,
you see that we have no power of ourselves to help ourselves:
keep us both outwardly in our bodies,
and inwardly in our souls;
that we may be defended from all adversities
  which may happen to the body,
and from all evil thoughts
  which may assault and hurt the soul;
through Jesus Christ our Lord.

Principal Service
Genesis 17.1-7,15-16
Psalm 22.23-31
Romans 4.13-25
Mark 8.31-38

Second Service
Psalm 135 *or* 135.1-14
Genesis 12.1-9
Hebrews 11.1-3,8-16
If the Second Service is a Eucharist, the following is read as a Gospel:
John 8.51-59

Third Service
Psalm 105.1-6,37-45
Isaiah 51.1-11
Galatians 3.1-9,23-29

The Annunciation of our Lord to the Blessed Virgin Mary

Saturday 25 March 2000 *Gold or White*

Collect†

We beseech you, O Lord,
pour your grace into our hearts,
that as we have known the incarnation
of your Son Jesus Christ
by the message of an angel,
so by his cross and passion
we may be brought to the glory of his resurrection;
through Jesus Christ your Son our Lord,
who is alive and reigns with you,
in the unity of the Holy Spirit,
one God, now and for ever.

Post Communion

God most high,
whose handmaid bore the Word made flesh:
we thank you that in this sacrament of our redemption
you visit us with your Holy Spirit
and overshadow us by your power;
strengthen us to walk with Mary the joyful path of obedience
and so to bring forth the fruits of holiness;
through Jesus Christ our Lord.

Evening Prayer on the Eve (24 March)
Psalm 85
Wisdom 9.1-12 *or* Genesis 3.8-15
Galatians 4.1-5

Eucharist
Isaiah 7.10-14
Psalm 40.5-10
Hebrews 10.4-10
Luke 1.26-38

Morning Prayer
Psalms 111, 113
1 Samuel 2.1-10
Romans 5.12-21

Evening Prayer
Psalms 131, 146
Isaiah 52.1-12
Hebrews 2.5-18

The Third Sunday of Lent

26 March 2000 *Purple or Lent Array*

Collect

Almighty God,
whose most dear Son went not up to joy
but first he suffered pain,
and entered not into glory before he was crucified:
mercifully grant that we, walking in the way of the cross,
may find it none other than the way of life and peace;
through Jesus Christ your Son our Lord,
who is alive and reigns with you,
in the unity of the Holy Spirit,
one God, now and for ever.

Post Communion†

Merciful Lord,
grant your people grace to withstand the temptations
of the world, the flesh and the devil,
and with pure hearts and minds to follow you,
the only God;
through Jesus Christ our Lord.

Principal Service
Exodus 20.1-17
Psalm 19 *or* 19.7-14
1 Corinthians 1.18-25
John 2.13-22

Second Service
Psalms 11, 12
Exodus 5.1 – 6.1
Philippians 3.4b-14 *or* Matthew 10.16-22

Third Service
Psalm 18.1-24
Jeremiah 38
Philippians 1.1-26

The Fourth Sunday of Lent

2 April 2000 *Purple or Lent Array*

Collect†

Merciful Lord,
absolve your people from their offences,
that through your bountiful goodness
we may all be delivered from the chains of those sins
which by our frailty we have committed;
grant this, heavenly Father,
for Jesus Christ's sake, our blessed Lord and Saviour,
who is alive and reigns with you,
in the unity of the Holy Spirit,
one God, now and for ever.

Post Communion

Lord God,
whose blessed Son our Saviour
gave his back to the smiters
and did not hide his face from shame:
give us grace to endure the sufferings of this present time
with sure confidence in the glory that shall be revealed;
through Jesus Christ our Lord.

Mothering Sunday may be observed in preference to any one of the provisions for the Fourth Sunday of Lent.

Principal Service

Numbers 21.4-9
Psalm 107.1-3,17-22 *or* 107.1-9
Ephesians 2.1-10
John 3.14-21

Second Service

Psalms 13, 14
Exodus 6.2-13
Romans 5.1-11
If the Second Service is a Eucharist, the following is read as a Gospel:
John 12.1-8

If the Principal Service readings have been displaced by the Mothering Sunday readings, they may be used at this service.

Third Service

Psalm 27
1 Samuel 16.1-13
John 9.1-25

Mothering Sunday

2 April 2000 ***Purple or Lent Array***

Collect

God of compassion,
whose Son Jesus Christ, the child of Mary,
shared the life of a home in Nazareth,
and on the cross drew the whole human family to himself:
strengthen us in our daily living
that in joy and in sorrow
we may know the power of your presence
to bind together and to heal;
through Jesus Christ your Son our Lord,
who is alive and reigns with you,
in the unity of the Holy Spirit,
one God, now and for ever.

Post Communion

Loving God,
as a mother feeds her children at the breast
you feed us in this sacrament
with the food and drink of eternal life:
help us who have tasted your goodness
to grow in grace within the household of faith;
through Jesus Christ our Lord.

Mothering Sunday may be observed in preference to any one of the provisions for the Fourth Sunday of Lent.

Exodus 2.1-10 *or* 1 Samuel 1.20-28
Psalm 34.11-20 *or* Psalm 127.1-4
2 Corinthians 1.3-7 *or* Colossians 3.12-17
Luke 2.33-35 *or* John 19.25-27

The Fifth Sunday of Lent

9 April 2000 *Purple or Lent Array*

Collect

Most merciful God,
who by the death and resurrection of your Son Jesus Christ
delivered and saved the world:
grant that by faith in him who suffered on the cross
we may triumph in the power of his victory;
through Jesus Christ your Son our Lord,
who is alive and reigns with you,
in the unity of the Holy Spirit,
one God, now and for ever.

Post Communion

Lord Jesus Christ,
you have taught us
that what we do for the least of our brothers and sisters
we do also for you:
give us the will to be the servant of others
as you were the servant of all,
and gave up your life and died for us,
but are alive and reign, now and for ever.

Principal Service

Jeremiah 31.31-34
Psalm 51.1-12 *or* Psalm 119.9-16
Hebrews 5.5-10
John 12.20-33

Second Service

Psalm 34 *or* 34.1-10
Exodus 7.8-24
Romans 5.12-21
If the Second Service is a Eucharist,
the following is read as a Gospel:
Luke 22.1-13

Third Service

Psalm 107.1-22
Exodus 24.3-8
Hebrews 12.18-29

Palm Sunday

16 April 2000 *Red*

Collect†

Almighty and everlasting God,
who in your tender love towards the human race
  sent your Son our Saviour Jesus Christ
to take upon him our flesh
and to suffer death upon the cross:
grant that we may follow the example
  of his patience and humility,
and also be made partakers of his resurrection;
through Jesus Christ your Son our Lord,
who is alive and reigns with you,
in the unity of the Holy Spirit,
one God, now and for ever.

Post Communion

Lord Jesus Christ,
you humbled yourself in taking the form of a servant,
and in obedience died on the cross for our salvation:
give us the mind to follow you
and to proclaim you as Lord and King,
to the glory of God the Father.

Principal Service
Liturgy of the Palms:
Mark 11.1-11 *or* John 12.12-16
Psalm 118.1-2,19-24 *or* 118.19-24

Liturgy of the Passion:
Isaiah 50.4-9a
Psalm 31.9-16[17-18]
Philippians 2.5-11
Mark 14.1 – 15.47 *or* 15.1-39[40-47]

Second Service
Psalm 69.1-18
Isaiah 5.1-7
Mark 12.1-12

Third Service
Psalms 61, 62
Zechariah 9.9-12
1 Corinthians 2.1-12

Maundy Thursday

20 April 2000 ***White***

Collect

God our Father,
you have invited us to share in the supper
which your Son gave to his Church
to proclaim his death until he comes:
may he nourish us by his presence,
and unite us in his love;
who is alive and reigns with you,
in the unity of the Holy Spirit,
one God, now and for ever.

At Morning and Evening Prayer the Collect of Palm Sunday is used.

Post Communion

Lord Jesus Christ,
we thank you that in this wonderful sacrament
you have given us the memorial of your passion:
grant us so to reverence the sacred mysteries
of your body and blood
that we may know within ourselves
and show forth in our lives
the fruit of your redemption,
for you are alive and reign, now and for ever.

Principal Service
Exodus 12.1-4[5-10]11-14
Psalm 116.1-2,12-19 *or* 116.11-19
1 Corinthians 11.23-26
John 13.1-17,31b-35

Second Service
Psalm 39
Leviticus 16.2-24
Luke 23.1-25

Third Service
Psalms 42, 43
Exodus 11
Ephesians 2.11-18

Good Friday

21 April 2000 ***Hangings removed: Red for the Liturgy***

Collect[†]

Almighty Father,
look with mercy on this your family
for which our Lord Jesus Christ
was content to be betrayed
and given up into the hands of sinners
and to suffer death upon the cross;
who is alive and glorified
with you and the Holy Spirit,
one God, now and for ever.

Principal Service
Isaiah 52.13 – 53.12
Psalm 22 *or* 22.1-11 *or* 22.1-21
Hebrews 10.16-25 *or* 4.14-16; 5.7-9
John 18.1 – 19.42

Second Service
Psalms 130, 143
Genesis 22.1-18
A part of John 18-19
if not used at the Principal Service
especially in the evening,
John 19.38-42 *or* Colossians 1.18-23

Third Service
Psalm 69
Lamentations 5.15-22
A part of John 18-19
if not read at the Principal Service
or Hebrews 10.1-10

Easter Eve

Saturday 22 April 2000 ***Hangings removed***

Collect[†]

Grant, Lord,
that we who are baptised into the death
of your Son our Saviour Jesus Christ
may continually put to death our evil desires
and be buried with him;
and that through the grave and gate of death
we may pass to our joyful resurrection;
through his merits, who died and was buried
and rose again for us,
your Son Jesus Christ our Lord.

These readings are for use at services other than the Easter Vigil.

Principal Service

Job 14.1-14 *or* Lamentations 3.1-9,19-24
Psalm 31.1-4,15-16 *or* 31.1-5
1 Peter 4.1-8
Matthew 27.57-66 *or* John 19.38-42

Second Service

Psalm 142
Hosea 6.1-6
John 2.18-22

Third Service

Psalm 116
Job 19.21-27
1 John 5.5-12

Easter Vigil

Saturday 22 / Sunday 23 April 2000 *Gold or White*

When the Eucharist is celebrated at this service, the Collect and Post Communion for Easter Day are used.

A minimum of three Old Testament readings (including Exodus 14) must be used, together with the Romans reading and the Gospel.

Genesis 1.1 – 2.4a	Psalm 136.1-9,23-26
Genesis 7.1-5,11-18; 8.6-18; 9.8-13	Psalm 46
Genesis 22.1-18	Psalm 16
Exodus 14.10-31; 15.20-21	***Canticle:* Exodus 15.1b-13,17-18**
Isaiah 55.1-11	*Canticle:* Isaiah 12.2-6
Baruch 3.9-15,32 – 4.4 *or* Proverbs 8.1-8,19-21; 9.4b-6	Psalm 19
Ezekiel 36.24-28	Psalms 42, 43
Ezekiel 37.1-14	Psalm 143
Zephaniah 3.14-20	Psalm 98
Romans 6.3-11	**Psalm 114**
Mark 16.1-8	

Easter Day

Sunday 23 April 2000 *Gold or White*

Collect

Lord of all life and power,
who through the mighty resurrection of your Son
overcame the old order of sin and death
to make all things new in him:
grant that we, being dead to sin
and alive to you in Jesus Christ,
may reign with him in glory;
to whom with you and the Holy Spirit
be praise and honour, glory and might,
now and in all eternity.

Post Communion

God of Life,
who for our redemption gave your only-begotten Son
to the death of the cross,
and by his glorious resurrection
have delivered us from the power of our enemy:
grant us so to die daily to sin,
that we may evermore live with him
in the joy of his risen life;
through Jesus Christ our Lord.

*The liturgical colour is **White** throughout Easter.*

Principal Service
Acts 10.34-43 *or* Isaiah 25.6-9
Psalm 118.[1-2]14-24
1 Corinthians 15.1-11 *or* Acts 10.34-43
John 20.1-18 *or* Mark 16.1-8

Second Service
Psalms 114, 117
Ezekiel 37.1-14
Luke 24.13-35

Third Service
Psalm 105 *or* 66.1-12
Genesis 1.1-5,26-31
2 Corinthians 5.14 – 6.2

The Second Sunday of Easter

30 April 2000 *White*

Collect†

Almighty Father,
you have given your only Son to die for our sins
and to rise again for our justification:
grant us so to put away the leaven of malice and wickedness
that we may always serve you
in pureness of living and truth;
through the merits of your Son Jesus Christ our Lord,
who is alive and reigns with you,
in the unity of the Holy Spirit,
one God, now and for ever.

Post Communion

Lord God our Father,
through our Saviour Jesus Christ
you have assured your children of eternal life
and in baptism have made us one with him:
deliver us from the death of sin
and raise us to new life in your love,
in the fellowship of the Holy Spirit,
by the grace of our Lord Jesus Christ.

Principal Service

	or if an Old Testament reading is required:
Acts 4.32-35	Exodus 14.10-31; 15.20-21
Psalm 133	Psalm 133
1 John 1.1 – 2.2	Acts 4.32-35
John 20.19-31	John 20.19-31

Second Service

Psalm 143.1-11
Isaiah 26.1-9,19
Luke 24.1-12

Third Service

Psalm 22.20-31
Isaiah 53.6-12
Romans 4.13-25

The Third Sunday of Easter

7 May 2000 *White*

Collect

Almighty Father,
who in your great mercy gladdened the disciples
with the sight of the risen Lord:
give us such knowledge of his presence with us,
that we may be strengthened and sustained
by his risen life
and serve you continually in righteousness and truth;
through Jesus Christ your Son our Lord,
who is alive and reigns with you,
in the unity of the Holy Spirit,
one God, now and for ever.

Post Communion

Living God,
your Son made himself known to his disciples
in the breaking of bread:
open the eyes of our faith,
that we may see him in all his redeeming work;
who is alive and reigns, now and for ever.

Principal Service

	or if an Old Testament reading is required:
Acts 3.12-19	Zephaniah 3.14-20
Psalm 4	Psalm 4
1 John 3.1-7	Acts 3.12-19
Luke 24.36b-48	Luke 24.36b-48

Second Service

Psalm 142
Deuteronomy 7.7-13
Revelation 2.1-11
If the Second Service is a Eucharist, the following is read as a Gospel:
Luke 16.19-31

Third Service

Psalm 77.11-20
Isaiah 63.7-15
1 Corinthians 10.1-13

The Fourth Sunday of Easter

14 May 2000 ***White***

Collect

Almighty God,
whose Son Jesus Christ is the resurrection and the life:
raise us, who trust in him,
from the death of sin to the life of righteousness,
that we may seek those things which are above,
where he reigns with you
in the unity of the Holy Spirit,
one God, now and for ever.

Post Communion

Merciful Father,
you gave your Son Jesus Christ to be the good shepherd,
and in his love for us to lay down his life and rise again:
keep us always under his protection,
and give us grace to follow in his steps;
through Jesus Christ our Lord.

Principal Service

	or if an Old Testament reading is required:
Acts 4.5-12	Genesis 7.1-5,11-18; 8.6-18; 9.8-13
Psalm 23	Psalm 23
1 John 3.16-24	Acts 4.5-12
John 10.11-18	John 10.11-18

Second Service

Psalm 81.8-16
Exodus 16.4-15
Revelation 2.12-17
If the Second Service is a Eucharist, the following is read as a Gospel:
John 6.30-40

Third Service

Psalm 119.89-96
Nehemiah 8.1-12
Luke 24.25-32

The Fifth Sunday of Easter

21 May 2000 *White*

Collect[†]

Almighty God,
who through your only-begotten Son Jesus Christ
have overcome death and opened to us
  the gate of everlasting life:
grant that, as by your grace going before us
  you put into our minds good desires,
so by your continual help
we may bring them to good effect;
through Jesus Christ our risen Lord,
who is alive and reigns with you,
in the unity of the Holy Spirit,
one God, now and for ever.

Post Communion

Eternal God,
whose Son Jesus Christ is the way, the truth, and the life:
grant us to walk in his way,
to rejoice in his truth,
and to share his risen life;
who is alive and reigns, now and for ever.

Principal Service

Acts 8.26-40
Psalm 22.25-31
1 John 4.7-21
John 15.1-8

or if an Old Testament reading is required:
Baruch 3.9-15,32 – 4.4 *or* Genesis 22.1-18
Psalm 22.25-31
Acts 8.26-40
John 15.1-8

Second Service

Psalm 96
Isaiah 60.1-14
Revelation 3.1-13
If the Second Service is a Eucharist, the following is read as a Gospel:
Mark 16.9-16

Third Service

Psalm 44.15-27
2 Maccabees 7.7-14 *or* Daniel 3.16-28
Hebrews 11.32 – 12.2

The Sixth Sunday of Easter

28 May 2000 *White*

Collect

God our redeemer,
you have delivered us from the power of darkness
and brought us into the kingdom of your Son:
grant, that as by his death he has recalled us to life,
so by his continual presence in us he may raise us
to eternal joy;
through Jesus Christ your Son our Lord,
who is alive and reigns with you,
in the unity of the Holy Spirit,
one God, now and for ever.

Post Communion

God our Father,
whose Son Jesus Christ gives the water of eternal life:
may we thirst for you,
the spring of life and source of goodness,
through him who is alive and reigns, now and for ever.

Principal Service

	or if an Old Testament reading is required:
Acts 10.44-48	Isaiah 55.1-11
Psalm 98	Psalm 98
1 John 5.1-6	Acts 10.44-48
John 15.9-17	John 15.9-17

Second Service

Psalm 45
Song of Solomon 4.16 – 5.2; 8.6-7
Revelation 3.14-22
If the Second Service is a Eucharist,
the following is read as a Gospel:
Luke 22.24-30

Third Service

Psalm 104.26-32
Ezekiel 47.1-12
John 21.1-19

Ascension Day

Thursday 1 June 2000 *Gold or White*

Collect[†]

Grant, we pray, almighty God,
that as we believe your only-begotten Son
our Lord Jesus Christ
to have ascended into the heavens,
so we in heart and mind may also ascend
and with him continually dwell;
who is alive and reigns with you,
in the unity of the Holy Spirit,
one God, now and for ever.

Post Communion

God our Father,
you have raised our humanity in Christ
and have fed us with the bread of heaven:
mercifully grant that, nourished with such spiritual blessings,
we may set our hearts in the heavenly places;
through Jesus Christ our Lord.

Evening Prayer on the Eve (31 May)
Psalms 15, 24
2 Samuel 23.1-5
Colossians 2.20 – 3.4

Principal Service
Acts 1.1-11 *or* Daniel 7.9-14
Psalm 47 *or* Psalm 93
Ephesians 1.15-23 *or* Acts 1.1-11
Luke 24.44-53
The reading from Acts must be used as either the first or second reading.

Second Service
Psalm 8
Song of the Three 29-37 *or* 2 Kings 2.1-15
Revelation 5
If the Second Service is a Eucharist, the following is read as a Gospel:
Matthew 28.16-20

Third Service
Psalm 110
Isaiah 52.7-15
Hebrews 7.11-28 *or* 7.26-28

The Seventh Sunday of Easter

Sunday after Ascension Day

4 June 2000 ***White***

Collect†

O God the king of glory,
you have exalted your only Son Jesus Christ
with great triumph to your kingdom in heaven:
we beseech you, leave us not comfortless,
but send your Holy Spirit to strengthen us
and exalt us to the place
  where our Saviour Christ is gone before,
who is alive and reigns with you,
in the unity of the Holy Spirit,
one God, now and for ever.

Post Communion

Eternal God, giver of love and power,
your Son Jesus Christ has sent us into all the world
to preach the gospel of his kingdom:
confirm us in this mission,
and help us to live the good news we proclaim;
through Jesus Christ our Lord.

Principal Service

	or if an Old Testament reading is required:
Acts 1.15-17,21-26	Ezekiel 36.24-28
Psalm 1	Psalm 1
1 John 5.9-13	Acts 1.15-17,21-26
John 17.6-19	John 17.6-19

Second Service

Psalm 147.1-11
Isaiah 61.1-11
Luke 4.14-21

Third Service

Psalm 76
Isaiah 14.3-15
Revelation 14.1-13

Day of Pentecost (Whit Sunday)

11 June 2000 *Red*

Collect[†]

God, who as at this time
taught the hearts of your faithful people
by sending to them the light of your Holy Spirit:
grant us by the same Spirit
to have a right judgement in all things
and evermore to rejoice in his holy comfort;
through the merits of Christ Jesus our Saviour,
who is alive and reigns with you,
in the unity of the Holy Spirit,
one God, now and for ever.

Post Communion

Faithful God,
who fulfilled the promises of Easter
by sending us your Holy Spirit
and opening to every race and nation
the way of life eternal:
open our lips by your Spirit,
that every tongue may tell of your glory;
through Jesus Christ our Lord.

This Collect and Post Communion are not used on the weekdays after Pentecost *(see page 65)**.*

Evening Prayer on the Eve (10 June)
Psalm 48
Deuteronomy 16.9-15
John 7.37-39

Principal Service
Acts 2.1-21 *or* Ezekiel 37.1-14
Psalm 104.24-34,35b *or* 104.24-36
Romans 8.22-27 *or* Acts 2.1-21
John 15.26-27; 16.4b-15
The reading from Acts must be used as either the first or second reading.

Second Service
Psalm 139.1-12[13-18,23-24]
Ezekiel 36.22-28
Acts 2.22-38
If the Second Service is a Eucharist, the following is read as a Gospel:
John 20.19-23

Third Service
Psalm 145
Isaiah 11.1-9
or Wisdom 7.15-23[24-27]
1 Corinthians 12.4-13

The Weekdays After the Day of Pentecost

Monday 12 – Saturday 17 June 2000 *Green*
except where other provision is made

Collect[†]

O Lord, from whom all good things come:
grant to us your humble servants,
that by your holy inspiration
we may think those things that are good,
and by your merciful guiding may perform the same;
through our Lord Jesus Christ,
who is alive and reigns with you,
in the unity of the Holy Spirit,
one God, now and for ever.

Post Communion

Gracious God, lover of all,
in this sacrament
we are one family in Christ your Son,
one in the sharing of his body and blood
and one in the communion of his Spirit:
help us to grow in love for one another
and come to the full maturity of the Body of Christ.
We make our prayer through your Son our Saviour.

The liturgical colour is ***Green*** *from the Monday after the feast of Pentecost until the Eve of All Saints' Day, except when other provision is made.*

Trinity Sunday

18 June 2000 *Gold or White*

Collect†

Almighty and everlasting God,
you have given us your servants grace,
by the confession of a true faith,
to acknowledge the glory of the eternal Trinity
and in the power of the divine majesty to worship the Unity:
keep us steadfast in this faith,
that we may evermore be defended from all adversities;
through Jesus Christ your Son our Lord,
who is alive and reigns with you,
in the unity of the Holy Spirit,
one God, now and for ever.

Post Communion

Almighty and eternal God,
you have revealed yourself as Father, Son and Holy Spirit,
and live and reign in the perfect unity of love:
hold us firm in this faith,
that we may know you in all your ways
and evermore rejoice in your eternal glory,
who are three Persons yet one God,
now and for ever.

Evening Prayer on the Eve (17 June)
Psalms 97, 98
Isaiah 40.12-31
Mark 1.1-13

Principal Service
Isaiah 6.1-8
Psalm 29
Romans 8.12-17
John 3.1-17

Second Service
Psalm 104.1-9
Ezekiel 1.4-10,22-28a
Revelation 4.1-11
If the Second Service is a Eucharist, the following is read as a Gospel:
Mark 1.1-13

Third Service
Psalm 33.1-12
Proverbs 8.1-4,22-31
2 Corinthians 13.[5-10]11-13

The First Sunday After Trinity

25 June 2000 ***Green***

Collect†

O God,
the strength of all those who put their trust in you,
mercifully accept our prayers
and, because through the weakness of our mortal nature
we can do no good thing without you,
grant us the help of your grace,
that in the keeping of your commandments
we may please you both in will and deed;
through Jesus Christ your Son our Lord,
who is alive and reigns with you,
in the unity of the Holy Spirit,
one God, now and for ever.

Post Communion

Eternal Father,
we thank you for nourishing us
with these heavenly gifts:
may our communion strengthen us in faith,
build us up in hope,
and make us grow in love;
for the sake of Jesus Christ our Lord.

PROPER 7

Principal Service

CONTINUOUS
1 Samuel 17.[1a,4-11,19-23]32-49
Psalm 9.9-20
Or:
1 Samuel 17.57 – 18.5,10-16
Psalm 133
2 Corinthians 6.1-13
Mark 4.35-41

RELATED
Job 38.1-11
Psalm 107.[1-3]23-32
2 Corinthians 6.1-13
Mark 4.35-41

Second Service
Psalm 49
Jeremiah 10.1-16
Romans 11.25-36
If the Second Service is a Eucharist, the following is read as a Gospel:
Luke 8.26-39

Third Service
Psalm 48
Deuteronomy 11.1-15
Acts 27.1-12

The Second Sunday After Trinity

2 July 2000 *Green*

Collect†

Lord, you have taught us
that all our doings without love are nothing worth:
send your Holy Spirit
and pour into our hearts that most excellent gift of love,
the true bond of peace and of all virtues,
without which whoever lives is counted dead before you.
Grant this for your only Son Jesus Christ's sake,
who is alive and reigns with you,
in the unity of the Holy Spirit,
one God, now and for ever.

Post Communion

Loving Father,
we thank you for feeding us at the supper of your Son:
sustain us with your Spirit,
that we may serve you here on earth
until our joy is complete in heaven,
and we share in the eternal banquet
with Jesus Christ our Lord.

PROPER 8

Principal Service

CONTINUOUS	RELATED
2 Samuel 1.1,17-27	Wisdom of Solomon 1.13-15; 2.23-24 *or* Lamentations 3.23-33
Psalm 130	*Canticle:* Lamentations 3.23-33 *or* Psalm 30
2 Corinthians 8.7-15	2 Corinthians 8.7-15
Mark 5.21-43	Mark 5.21-43

Second Service

Psalms [52] 53
Jeremiah 11.1-14
Romans 13.1-10
If the Second Service is a Eucharist, the following is read as a Gospel:
Luke 9.51-62

Third Service

Psalm 56
Deuteronomy 15.1-11
Acts 27.[13-32]33-44

The Third Sunday After Trinity

9 July 2000 *Green*

Collect

Almighty God,
you have broken the tyranny of sin
and have sent the Spirit of your Son into our hearts
whereby we call you Father:
give us grace to dedicate our freedom to your service,
that we and all creation may be brought
to the glorious liberty of the children of God;
through Jesus Christ your Son our Lord,
who is alive and reigns with you,
in the unity of the Holy Spirit,
one God, now and for ever.

Post Communion

O God, whose beauty is beyond our imagining
and whose power we cannot comprehend:
show us your glory as far as we can grasp it,
and shield us from knowing more than we can bear
until we may look upon you without fear;
through Jesus Christ our Saviour.

PROPER 9

Principal Service

Continuous	Related
2 Samuel 5.1-5,9-10	Ezekiel 2.1-5
Psalm 48	Psalm 123
2 Corinthians 12.2-10	2 Corinthians 12.2-10
Mark 6.1-13	Mark 6.1-13

Second Service

Psalms [63] 64
Jeremiah 20.1-11a
Romans 14.1-17
If the Second Service is a Eucharist, the following is read as a Gospel:
Luke 10.1-11,16-20

Third Service

Psalm 57
Deuteronomy 24.10-22
Acts 28.1-16

The Fourth Sunday After Trinity

16 July 2000 *Green*

Collect†

O God, the protector of all who trust in you,
without whom nothing is strong, nothing is holy:
increase and multiply upon us your mercy;
that with you as our ruler and guide
we may so pass through things temporal
that we lose not our hold on things eternal;
grant this, heavenly Father,
for our Lord Jesus Christ's sake,
who is alive and reigns with you,
in the unity of the Holy Spirit,
one God, now and for ever.

Post Communion

Eternal God,
comfort of the afflicted and healer of the broken,
you have fed us at the table of life and hope:
teach us the ways of gentleness and peace,
that all the world may acknowledge
the kingdom of your Son Jesus Christ our Lord.

PROPER 10

Principal Service

CONTINUOUS	RELATED
2 Samuel 6.1-5,12b-19	Amos 7.7-15
Psalm 24	Psalm 85.8-13
Ephesians 1.3-14	Ephesians 1.3-14
Mark 6.14-29	Mark 6.14-29

Second Service
Psalm 66 *or* 66.1-9
Job 4.1; 5.6-27 *or* Ecclesiasticus 4.11-31
Romans 15.14-29
If the Second Service is a Eucharist,
the following is read as a Gospel:
Luke 10.25-37

Third Service
Psalm 65
Deuteronomy 28.1-14
Acts 28.17-30

The Fifth Sunday After Trinity

23 July 2000 *Green*

Collect†

Almighty and everlasting God,
by whose Spirit the whole body of the Church
  is governed and sanctified:
hear our prayer which we offer for all your faithful people,
that in their vocation and ministry
they may serve you in holiness and truth
to the glory of your name;
through our Lord and Saviour Jesus Christ,
who is alive and reigns with you,
in the unity of the Holy Spirit,
one God, now and for ever.

Post Communion†

Grant, O Lord, we beseech you,
that the course of this world may be so peaceably ordered
  by your governance,
that your Church may joyfully serve you
  in all godly quietness;
through Jesus Christ our Lord.

PROPER 11

Principal Service

Continuous	Related
2 Samuel 7.1-14a	Jeremiah 23.1-6
Psalm 89.20-37	Psalm 23
Ephesians 2.11-22	Ephesians 2.11-22
Mark 6.30-34,53-56	Mark 6.30-34,53-56

Second Service

Psalm 73 *or* 73.21-28
Job 13.13 – 14.6 *or* Ecclesiasticus 18.1-14
Hebrews 2.5-18
If the Second Service is a Eucharist, the following is read as a Gospel:
Luke 10.38-42

Third Service

Psalms 67, 70
Deuteronomy 30.1-10
1 Peter 3.8-18

The Sixth Sunday After Trinity

30 July 2000 *Green*

Collect†

Merciful God,
you have prepared for those who love you
such good things as pass our understanding:
pour into our hearts such love toward you
that we, loving you in all things and above all things,
may obtain your promises,
which exceed all that we can desire;
through Jesus Christ your Son our Lord,
who is alive and reigns with you,
in the unity of the Holy Spirit,
one God, now and for ever.

Post Communion

God of our pilgrimage,
you have led us to the living water:
refresh and sustain us
as we go forward on our journey,
in the name of Jesus Christ our Lord.

PROPER 12

Principal Service

CONTINUOUS	RELATED
2 Samuel 11.1-15	2 Kings 4.42-44
Psalm 14	Psalm 145.10-18
Ephesians 3.14-21	Ephesians 3.14-21
John 6.1-21	John 6.1-21

Second Service

Psalm 74 *or* 74.12-17
Job 19.1-27a *or* Ecclesiasticus 38.24-34
Hebrews 8
If the Second Service is a Eucharist,
the following is read as a Gospel:
Luke 11.1-13

Third Service

Psalm 75
Song of Solomon 2
or 1 Maccabees 2.[1-14]15-22
1 Peter 4.7-14

The Transfiguration of Our Lord

6 August 2000 *Gold or White*

Collect

Father in heaven,
whose Son Jesus Christ was wonderfully transfigured
before chosen witnesses upon the holy mountain,
and spoke of the exodus he would accomplish at Jerusalem:
give us strength so to hear his voice and bear our cross
that in the world to come we may see him as he is;
who is alive and reigns with you,
in the unity of the Holy Spirit,
one God, now and for ever.

Post Communion

Holy God,
we see your glory in the face of Jesus Christ:
may we who are partakers at his table
reflect his life in word and deed,
that all the world may know
his power to change and save.
This we ask through Jesus Christ our Lord.

The Transfiguration is celebrated on the Sixth Sunday after Trinity (6 August) unless transferred to Monday 7 August.

Evening Prayer on the Eve, if required (5 August)
Psalms 99, 110
Exodus 24.12-18
John 12.27-36a

Eucharist
Daniel 7.9-10,13-14
Psalm 97
2 Peter 1.16-19
Luke 9.28-36

Morning Prayer
Psalm 27
Ecclesiasticus 48.1-10
or 1 Kings 19.1-16
1 John 3.1-3

Evening Prayer
Psalm 72
Exodus 34.29-35
2 Corinthians 3

The Seventh Sunday After Trinity

6 August 2000 *Green*

Collect†

Lord of all power and might,
the author and giver of all good things:
graft in our hearts the love of your name,
increase in us true religion,
nourish us with all goodness,
and of your great mercy keep us in the same;
through Jesus Christ your Son our Lord,
who is alive and reigns with you,
in the unity of the Holy Spirit,
one God, now and for ever.

Post Communion

Lord God, whose Son is the true vine and the source of life,
ever giving himself that the world may live:
may we so receive within ourselves
  the power of his death and passion
that, in his saving cup,
  we may share his glory and be made perfect in his love;
for he is alive and reigns, now and for ever.

This provision is used on 6 August only if the Transfiguration is transferred to Monday 7 August.

PROPER 13

Principal Service

CONTINUOUS	RELATED
2 Samuel 11.26 – 12.13a	Exodus 16.2-4,9-15
Psalm 51.1-12	Psalm 78.23-29
Ephesians 4.1-16	Ephesians 4.1-16
John 6.24-35	John 6.24-35

Second Service

Psalm 88 *or* 88.1-9
Job 28 *or* Ecclesiasticus 42.15-25
Hebrews 11.17-31
If the Second Service is a Eucharist, the following is read as a Gospel:
Luke 12.13-21

Third Service

Psalm 86
Song of Solomon 5.2-16
  or 1 Maccabees 3.1-12
2 Peter 1.1-15

The Eighth Sunday After Trinity

13 August 2000 *Green*

Collect†

Almighty Lord and everlasting God,
we beseech you to direct, sanctify and govern
  both our hearts and bodies
in the ways of your laws
  and the works of your commandments;
that through your most mighty protection, both here and ever,
we may be preserved in body and soul;
through our Lord and Saviour Jesus Christ,
who is alive and reigns with you,
in the unity of the Holy Spirit,
one God, now and for ever.

Post Communion

Strengthen for service, Lord,
the hands that have taken holy things;
may the ears which have heard your word
  be deaf to clamour and dispute;
may the tongues which have sung your praise
  be free from deceit;
may the eyes which have seen the tokens of your love
  shine with the light of hope;
and may the bodies which have been fed with your body
  be refreshed with the fullness of your life;
glory to you for ever.

PROPER 14

Principal Service

CONTINUOUS	RELATED
2 Samuel 18.5-9,15,31-33	1 Kings 19.4-8
Psalm 130	Psalm 34.1-8
Ephesians 4.25 – 5.2	Ephesians 4.25 – 5.2
John 6.35,41-51	John 6.35,41-51

Second Service

Psalm 91 *or* 91.1-12
Job 39.1 – 40.4
  or Ecclesiasticus 43.13-33
Hebrews 12.1-17
If the Second Service is a Eucharist, the following is read as a Gospel:
Luke 12.32-40

Third Service

Psalm 90
Song of Solomon 8.5-7
  or 1 Maccabees 14.4-15
2 Peter 3.8-13

The Ninth Sunday After Trinity

20 August 2000 *Green*

Collect

Almighty God,
who sent your Holy Spirit
to be the life and light of your Church:
open our hearts to the riches of your grace,
that we may bring forth the fruit of the Spirit
in love and joy and peace;
through Jesus Christ your Son our Lord,
who is alive and reigns with you,
in the unity of the Holy Spirit,
one God, now and for ever.

Post Communion

Holy Father,
who gathered us here around the table of your Son
to share this meal with the whole household of God:
in that new world
  where you reveal the fullness of your peace,
gather people of every race and language
  to share in the eternal banquet
  of Jesus Christ our Lord.

PROPER 15

Principal Service

CONTINUOUS	RELATED
1 Kings 2.10-12; 3.3-14	Proverbs 9.1-6
Psalm 111	Psalm 34.9-14
Ephesians 5.15-20	Ephesians 5.15-20
John 6.51-58	John 6.51-58

Second Service

Psalms [92] 100
Exodus 2.23 – 3.10
Hebrews 13.1-15
If the Second Service is a Eucharist, the following is read as a Gospel:
Luke 12.49-56

Third Service

Psalm 106.1-10
Jonah 1 *or* Ecclesiasticus 3.1-15
2 Peter 3.14-18

The Tenth Sunday After Trinity

27 August 2000 *Green*

Collect†

Let your merciful ears, O Lord,
be open to the prayers of your humble servants;
and that they may obtain their petitions
make them to ask such things as shall please you;
through Jesus Christ your Son our Lord,
who is alive and reigns with you,
in the unity of the Holy Spirit,
one God, now and for ever.

Post Communion

God of our pilgrimage,
you have willed that the gate of mercy
should stand open for those who trust in you:
look upon us with your favour
that we who follow the path of your will
may never wander from the way of life;
through Jesus Christ our Lord.

PROPER 16

Principal Service

CONTINUOUS	RELATED
1 Kings 8.[1,6,10-11]22-30,41-43	Joshua 24.1-2a,14-18
Psalm 84	Psalm 34.15-22
Ephesians 6.10-20	Ephesians 6.10-20
John 6.56-69	John 6.56-69

Second Service

Psalm 116 *or* 116.12-19
Exodus 4.27 – 5.1
Hebrews 13.16-21
If the Second Service is a Eucharist,
the following is read as a Gospel:
Luke 13.10-17

Third Service

Psalm 115
Jonah 2 *or* Ecclesiasticus 3.17-29
Revelation 1

The Eleventh Sunday After Trinity

3 September 2000 *Green*

Collect†

O God, you declare your almighty power
most chiefly in showing mercy and pity:
mercifully grant to us such a measure of your grace,
that we, running the way of your commandments,
may receive your gracious promises,
and be made partakers of your heavenly treasure;
through Jesus Christ your Son our Lord,
who is alive and reigns with you,
in the unity of the Holy Spirit,
one God, now and for ever.

Post Communion

Lord of all mercy,
we your faithful people have celebrated that one true sacrifice
which takes away our sins and brings pardon and peace:
by our communion
keep us firm on the foundation of the gospel
and preserve us from all sin;
through Jesus Christ our Lord.

PROPER 17

Principal Service

CONTINUOUS	RELATED
Song of Solomon 2.8-13	Deuteronomy 4.1-2,6-9
Psalm 45.1-2,6-9 *or* 45.1-7	Psalm 15
James 1.17-27	James 1.17-27
Mark 7.1-8,14-15,21-23	Mark 7.1-8,14-15,21-23

Second Service

Psalm 119.1-16 *or* 119.9-16
Exodus 12.21-27
Matthew 4.23 – 5.20

Third Service

Psalm 119.17-40
Jonah 3.1-9 *or* Ecclesiasticus 11.7-28
or 11.19-28
Revelation 3.14-22

The Twelfth Sunday After Trinity

10 September 2000 *Green*

Collect†

Almighty and everlasting God,
you are always more ready to hear than we to pray
and to give more than either we desire or deserve:
pour down upon us the abundance of your mercy,
forgiving us those things of which our conscience is afraid
and giving us those good things
   which we are not worthy to ask
but through the merits and mediation
of Jesus Christ your Son our Lord,
who is alive and reigns with you,
in the unity of the Holy Spirit,
one God, now and for ever.

Post Communion

God of all mercy,
in this eucharist you have set aside our sins
and given us your healing:
grant that we who are made whole in Christ
may bring that healing to this broken world,
in the name of Jesus Christ our Lord.

PROPER 18

Principal Service

Continuous	Related
Proverbs 22.1-2,8-9,22-23	Isaiah 35.4-7a
Psalm 125	Psalm 146
James 2.1-10[11-13]14-17	James 2.1-10[11-13]14-17
Mark 7.24-37	Mark 7.24-37

Second Service

Psalm 119.41-56 *or* 119.49-56
Exodus 14.5-31
Matthew 6.1-18

Third Service

Psalm 119.57-72
Jonah 3.10 – 4.11
   or Ecclesiasticus 27.30 – 28.9
Revelation 8.1-5

The Thirteenth Sunday After Trinity

17 September 2000 *Green*

Collect

Almighty God,
who called your Church to bear witness
that you were in Christ reconciling the world to yourself:
help us to proclaim the good news of your love,
that all who hear it may be drawn to you;
through him who was lifted up on the cross,
and reigns with you in the unity of the Holy Spirit,
one God, now and for ever.

Post Communion

God our creator,
you feed your children with the true manna,
the living bread from heaven:
let this holy food sustain us through our earthly pilgrimage
until we come to that place
   where hunger and thirst are no more;
through Jesus Christ our Lord.

PROPER 19

Principal Service

CONTINUOUS
Proverbs 1.20-33
Psalm 19 *or* 19.1-6
   or Canticle: Wisdom of
   Solomon 7.26 – 8.1
James 3.1-12
Mark 8.27-38

RELATED
Isaiah 50.4-9a
Psalm 116.1-9
James 3.1-12
Mark 8.27-38

Second Service

Psalm 119.73-88 *or* 119.73-80
Exodus 18.13-26
Matthew 7.1-14

Third Service

Psalm 119.105-120
Isaiah 44.24 – 45.8
Revelation 12.1-12

The Fourteenth Sunday After Trinity

24 September 2000 *Green*

Collect

Almighty God,
whose only Son has opened for us
a new and living way into your presence:
give us pure hearts and steadfast wills
to worship you in spirit and in truth;
through Jesus Christ your Son our Lord,
who is alive and reigns with you,
in the unity of the Holy Spirit,
one God, now and for ever.

Post Communion

Lord God, the source of truth and love,
keep us faithful to the apostles' teaching and fellowship,
united in prayer and the breaking of bread,
and one in joy and simplicity of heart,
in Jesus Christ our Lord.

PROPER 20

Principal Service

CONTINUOUS	RELATED
Proverbs 31.10-31	Wisdom of Solomon 1.16 – 2.1,12-22 *or* Jeremiah 11.18-20
Psalm 1	Psalm 54
James 3.13 – 4.3,7-8a	James 3.13 – 4.3,7-8a
Mark 9.30-37	Mark 9.30-37

Second Service

Psalm 119.137-152 *or* 119.137-144
Exodus 19.10-25
Matthew 8.23-34

Third Service

Psalm 119.153-176
Isaiah 45.9-22
Revelation 14.1-5

The Fifteenth Sunday After Trinity

1 October 2000 *Green*

Collect

God, who in generous mercy sent the Holy Spirit
upon your Church in the burning fire of your love:
grant that your people may be fervent
in the fellowship of the gospel
that, always abiding in you,
they may be found steadfast in faith and active in service;
through Jesus Christ your Son our Lord,
who is alive and reigns with you,
in the unity of the Holy Spirit,
one God, now and for ever.

Post Communion†

Keep, O Lord, your Church,
with your perpetual mercy;
and, because without you our human frailty cannot but fall,
keep us ever by your help from all things hurtful,
and lead us to all things profitable to our salvation;
through Jesus Christ our Lord.

The feast of Dedication may be celebrated in preference to the provision for the Fifteenth Sunday after Trinity or the Last Sunday after Trinity.

PROPER 21

Principal Service

Continuous	Related
Esther 7.1-6,9-10; 9.20-22	Numbers 11.4-6,10-16,24-29
Psalm 124	Psalm 19.7-14
James 5.13-20	James 5.13-20
Mark 9.38-50	Mark 9.38-50

Second Service

Psalms 120, 121
Exodus 24
Matthew 9.1-8

Third Service

Psalm 122
Isaiah 48.12-22
Luke 11.37-54

Dedication Festival

1 or 29 October 2000 *Gold or White*

Collect

Almighty God,
to whose glory we celebrate the dedication
of this house of prayer:
we praise you for the many blessings
you have given to those who worship you here:
and we pray that all who seek you in this place
may find you,
and, being filled with the Holy Spirit,
may become a living temple acceptable to you;
through Jesus Christ your Son our Lord,
who is alive and reigns with you,
in the unity of the Holy Spirit,
one God, now and for ever.

Post Communion

Father in heaven,
whose Church on earth is a sign of your heavenly peace,
an image of the new and eternal Jerusalem:
grant to us in the days of our pilgrimage
that, fed with the living bread of heaven,
and united in the body of your Son,
we may be the temple of your presence,
the place of your glory on earth,
and a sign of your peace in the world;
through Jesus Christ our Lord.

When the actual date is not known, the feast of Dedication may be celebrated in preference to the provision for the Fifteenth Sunday after Trinity or the Last Sunday after Trinity.

Evening Prayer on the Eve (30 September or 28 October)
Psalm 24
2 Chronicles 7.11-16
John 4.19-29

Principal Service
Genesis 28.11-18 *or* Revelation 21.9-14
Psalm 122
1 Peter 2.1-10
John 10.22-29

Second Service
Psalm 132
Jeremiah 7.1-11
Luke 19.1-10

Third Service
Psalm 48
Haggai 2.6-9
Hebrews 10.19-25

The Sixteenth Sunday After Trinity

8 October 2000 *Green*

Collect[†]

O Lord, we beseech you mercifully to hear the prayers
of your people who call upon you;
and grant that they may both perceive and know
what things they ought to do,
and also may have grace and power
faithfully to fulfil them;
through Jesus Christ your Son our Lord,
who is alive and reigns with you,
in the unity of the Holy Spirit,
one God, now and for ever.

Post Communion

Almighty God,
you have taught us through your Son
that love is the fulfilling of the law:
grant that we may love you with our whole heart
and our neighbours as ourselves;
through Jesus Christ our Lord.

PROPER 22

Principal Service

CONTINUOUS	RELATED
Job 1.1; 2.1-10	Genesis 2.18-24
Psalm 26	Psalm 8
Hebrews 1.1-4; 2.5-12	Hebrews 1.1-4; 2.5-12
Mark 10.2-16	Mark 10.2-16

Second Service

Psalms 125, 126
Joshua 3.7-17
Matthew 10.1-22

Third Service

Psalms 123, 124
Isaiah 49.13-23
Luke 12.1-12

The Seventeenth Sunday After Trinity

15 October 2000 *Green*

Collect

Almighty God,
you have made us for yourself,
and our hearts are restless till they find their rest in you:
pour your love into our hearts and draw us to yourself,
and so bring us at last to your heavenly city
where we shall see you face to face;
through Jesus Christ your Son our Lord,
who is alive and reigns with you,
in the unity of the Holy Spirit,
one God, now and for ever.

Post Communion†

Lord, we pray that your grace
  may always precede and follow us,
and make us continually to be given to all good works;
through Jesus Christ our Lord.

PROPER 23

Principal Service

CONTINUOUS	RELATED
Job 23.1-9,16-17	Amos 5.6-7,10-15
Psalm 22.1-15	Psalm 90.12-17
Hebrews 4.12-16	Hebrews 4.12-16
Mark 10.17-31	Mark 10.17-31

Second Service

Psalms 127 [128]
Joshua 5.13 – 6.20
Matthew 11.20-30

Third Service

Psalms 129, 130
Isaiah 50.4-10
Luke 13.22-30

The Eighteenth Sunday After Trinity

22 October 2000 *Green*

Collect

Almighty and everlasting God,
increase in us your gift of faith
that, forsaking what lies behind
and reaching out to that which is before,
we may run the way of your commandments
and win the crown of everlasting joy;
through Jesus Christ your Son our Lord,
who is alive and reigns with you,
in the unity of the Holy Spirit,
one God, now and for ever.

Post Communion

We praise and thank you, O Christ, for this sacred feast:
for here we receive you,
here the memory of your passion is renewed,
here our minds are filled with grace,
and here a pledge of future glory is given,
when we shall feast at that table where you reign
with all your saints for ever.

PROPER 24

Principal Service

CONTINUOUS	RELATED
Job 38.1-7[34-41]	Isaiah 53.4-12
Psalm 104.1-9[24,35c]	Psalm 91.9-16
Hebrews 5.1-10	Hebrews 5.1-10
Mark 10.35-45	Mark 10.35-45

Second Service

Psalm 141
Joshua 14.6-14
Matthew 12.1-21

Third Service

Psalms 133, 134, 137.1-6
Isaiah 54.1-14
Luke 13.31-35

The Last Sunday After Trinity

29 October 2000 *Green*

Collect[†]

Blessed Lord,
who caused all holy scriptures
to be written for our learning:
help us so to hear them,
to read, mark, learn and inwardly digest them
that, through patience, and the comfort of your holy word,
we may embrace and for ever hold fast
the hope of everlasting life,
which you have given us in our Saviour Jesus Christ,
who is alive and reigns with you,
in the unity of the Holy Spirit,
one God, now and for ever.

Post Communion

God of all grace,
your Son Jesus Christ fed the hungry
with the bread of his life
and the word of his kingdom:
renew your people with your heavenly grace,
and in all our weakness
sustain us by your true and living bread;
who is alive and reigns, now and for ever.

The feast of Dedication (see page 83) or Bible Sunday (see page 88) may be celebrated on this date.

PROPER 25

Principal Service

CONTINUOUS	RELATED
Job 42.1-6,10-17	Jeremiah 31.7-9
Psalm 34.1-8[19-22]	Psalm 126
Hebrews 7.23-28	Hebrews 7.23-28
Mark 10.46-52	Mark 10.46-52

Second Service	**Third Service**
Psalm 119.121-136	Psalm 119.89-104
Ecclesiastes 11, 12	Isaiah 59.9-20
2 Timothy 2.1-7	Luke 14.1-14
If the Second Service is a Eucharist, the following is read as a Gospel:	
Luke 18.9-14	

Bible Sunday

29 October 2000 *Green*

Collect†

Blessed Lord,
who caused all holy scriptures
to be written for our learning:
help us so to hear them,
to read, mark, learn and inwardly digest them
that, through patience, and the comfort of your holy word,
we may embrace and for ever hold fast
the hope of everlasting life,
which you have given us in our Saviour Jesus Christ,
who is alive and reigns with you,
in the unity of the Holy Spirit,
one God, now and for ever.

Post Communion

God of all grace,
your Son Jesus Christ fed the hungry
with the bread of his life
and the word of his kingdom:
renew your people with your heavenly grace,
and in all our weakness
sustain us by your true and living bread;
who is alive and reigns, now and for ever.

Bible Sunday may be celebrated in preference to the provision for the Last Sunday after Trinity (29 October).

Principal Service
Isaiah 55.1-11
Psalm 19.7-14
2 Timothy 3.14 – 4.5
John 5.36b-47

Second Service
Psalm 119.1-16
2 Kings 22
Colossians 3.12-17

Third Service
Psalm 119.89-104
Isaiah 45.22-45
Matthew 24.30-35 *or* Luke 14.1-14

All Saints' Day

Wednesday 1 November 2000 *Gold or White*

Collect†

Almighty God,
you have knit together your elect
in one communion and fellowship
in the mystical body of your Son Christ our Lord:
grant us grace so to follow your blessed saints
in all virtuous and godly living
that we may come to those inexpressible joys
that you have prepared for those who truly love you;
through Jesus Christ your Son our Lord,
who is alive and reigns with you,
in the unity of the Holy Spirit,
one God, now and for ever.

Post Communion

God, the source of all holiness
and giver of all good things:
may we who have shared at this table
as strangers and pilgrims here on earth
be welcomed with all your saints
to the heavenly feast on the day of your kingdom;
through Jesus Christ our Lord.

All Saints' Day may be celebrated on Sunday 5 November in preference to Wednesday 1 November, thus replacing the Fourth Sunday before Advent.
The liturgical colour is ***Green*** *or* ***Red*** *from after All Saints' Day to the Eve of the First Sunday of Advent, except when other provision is made.*

Evening Prayer on the Eve, if required (31 October)
Psalms 1, 5
Ecclesiasticus 44.1-15 *or* Isaiah 40.27-31
Revelation 19.6-10

Eucharist	Morning Prayer	Evening Prayer
Wisdom 3.1-9	Psalms 15, 84	Psalms 148, 150
or Isaiah 25.6-9	Isaiah 35.1-9	Isaiah 65.17-25
Psalm 24.1-6	Luke 9.18-27	Hebrews 11.32 – 12.2
Revelation 21.1-6a		
John 11.32-34		

If All Saints' Day is celebrated on Sunday 5 November, the following provision is used on 1 November.

Eucharist	Morning Prayer	Evening Prayer
Isaiah 56.3-8	Psalms 111, 112, 117	Psalm 145
or 2 Esdras 2.42-48	Wisdom 5.1-16	Isaiah 66.20-23
Psalm 33.1-5	*or* Jeremiah 31.31-34	Colossians 1.9-14
Hebrews 12.18-24	2 Corinthians 4.5-12	
Matthew 5.1-12		

The Fourth Sunday Before Advent

5 November 2000 *Red or Green*

Collect

Almighty and eternal God,
you have kindled the flame of love
in the hearts of the saints:
grant to us the same faith and power of love,
that, as we rejoice in their triumphs,
we may be sustained by their example and fellowship;
through Jesus Christ your Son our Lord,
who is alive and reigns with you,
in the unity of the Holy Spirit,
one God, now and for ever.

Post Communion

Lord of heaven,
in this eucharist you have brought us near
to an innumerable company of angels
and to the spirits of the saints made perfect:
as in this food of our earthly pilgrimage
we have shared their fellowship,
so may we come to share their joy in heaven;
through Jesus Christ our Lord.

All Saints' Day may be celebrated on Sunday 5 November in preference to Wednesday 1 November, thus replacing the Fourth Sunday before Advent.

Principal Service
Deuteronomy 6.1-9
Psalm 119.1-8
Hebrews 9.11-14
Mark 12.28-34

Second Service
Psalm 145 *or* 145.1-9
Daniel 2.1-48 *or* 2.1-11,25-48
Revelation 7.9-17
If the Second Service is a Eucharist, the following is read as a Gospel:
Matthew 5.1-12

Third Service
Psalms 112, 149
Jeremiah 31.31-34
1 John 3.1-3

The Third Sunday Before Advent

12 November 2000 *Red or Green*

Collect

Almighty Father,
whose will is to restore all things
in your beloved Son, the king of all:
govern the hearts and minds of those in authority,
and bring the families of the nations,
divided and torn apart by the ravages of sin,
to be subject to his just and gentle rule;
who is alive and reigns with you,
in the unity of the Holy Spirit,
one God, now and for ever.

Post Communion

God of peace,
whose Son Jesus Christ proclaimed the kingdom
and restored the broken to wholeness of life:
look with compassion on the anguish of the world,
and by your healing power
make whole both people and nations;
through our Lord and Saviour Jesus Christ.

Remembrance Sunday is observed on this day.

Principal Service
Jonah 3.1-5,10
Psalm 62.5-12
Hebrews 9.24-28
Mark 1.14-20

Second Service
Psalms 46 [82]
Isaiah 10.33 – 11.9
John 14.1-29 *or* 14.23-29

Third Service
Psalm 136
Micah 4.1-5
Philippians 4.6-9

The Second Sunday Before Advent

19 November 2000 *Red or Green*

Collect[†]

Heavenly Father,
whose blessed Son was revealed
to destroy the works of the devil
and to make us the children of God and heirs of eternal life:
grant that we, having this hope,
may purify ourselves even as he is pure;
that when he shall appear in power and great glory
we may be made like him
in his eternal and glorious kingdom;
where he is alive and reigns with you,
in the unity of the Holy Spirit,
one God, now and for ever.

Post Communion

Gracious Lord,
in this holy sacrament
you give substance to our hope:
bring us at the last
to that fullness of life for which we long;
through Jesus Christ our Saviour.

Principal Service
Daniel 12.1-3
Psalm 16
Hebrews 10.11-14[15-18]19-25
Mark 13.1-8

Second Service
Psalm 95
Daniel 3 *or* 3.13-30
Matthew 13.24-30,36-43

Third Service
Psalm 96
1 Samuel 9.27 – 10.2a; 10.17-26
Matthew 13.31-35

Harvest Thanksgiving

Green

Collect

Eternal God,
you crown the year with your goodness
and you give us the fruits of the earth in their season:
grant that we may use them to your glory,
  for the relief of those in need
  and for our own well-being;
through Jesus Christ your Son our Lord,
who is alive and reigns with you,
in the unity of the Holy Spirit,
one God, now and for ever.

Post Communion

Lord of the harvest,
with joy we have offered thanksgiving
  for your love in creation
and have shared in the bread and the wine of the kingdom:
by your grace plant within us a reverence for all that you give us
and make us generous and wise stewards
of the good things we enjoy;
through Jesus Christ our Lord.

Principal Service
Joel 2.21-27
Psalm 126
1 Timothy 2.1-7 *or* 1 Timothy 6.6-10
Matthew 6.25-33

Acknowledgements

The publisher gratefully acknowledges permission to reproduce copyright material in this book. Every effort has been made to trace and contact copyright holders. If there are any inadvertent omissions we apologize to those concerned.

The Consultation on Common Texts: *The Revised Common Lectionary* is copyright © The Consultation on Common Texts 1992. The Church of England adaptations to the Principal Service lectionary are copyright © The Archbishops' Council, as are the Second and Third Service lectionaries.

The Archbishops' Council: *The Alternative Service Book 1980; Lent, Holy Week, Easter,* 1986; *The Promise of His Glory,* 1991; *Patterns for Worship,* 1995; new compositions by the Liturgical Commission of the Church of England are copyright © The Archbishops' Council.

Cambridge University Press: Extracts adapted from *The Book of Common Prayer* (1662), the rights in which are vested in the Crown, are reproduced by permission of the Crown's Patentee, Cambridge University Press.

The Central Board of Finance of the Church of England: *The Prayer Book as Proposed in 1928* (additions and deviations).

General Synod of the Anglican Church of Canada: Based on (or excerpted from) *The Book of Alternative Services of the Anglican Church of Canada,* copyright © 1985. Used with permission.

International Commission on English in the Liturgy: The English translation from the collects and post communions from *The Roman Missal* © 1973, International Commission on English in the Liturgy, Inc. All rights reserved.

General Synod of the Church of Ireland: *Alternative Prayer Book 1984*; *Collects and Post-Communion Prayers,* 1995. Reproduced with permission.

Church of the Province of Southern Africa: *An Anglican Prayer Book 1989* © Provincial Trustees of the Church of the Province of Southern Africa (includes material from *Modern Collects,* 1972 and *Liturgy 75,* 1975).

Episcopal Church of the USA, *The Book of Common Prayer* according to the use of the Episcopal Church of the USA, 1979. The ECUSA Prayer Book is not subject to copyright.

Church in Wales Publications: *The Book of Common Prayer for use in the Church in Wales,* Vol.1, 1984. Used with permission.

Cassell plc: C L MacDonnell, *After Communion,* 1985; David Silk (ed.), *Prayers for use at the Alternative Services,* 1980; revised 1986 are copyright © Mowbray, an imprint of Cassell.

Hodder and Stoughton *Publishers*: Frank Colquhoun (ed.), *Parish Prayers,* Hodder and Stoughton, 1967.

Janet Morley: *All Desires Known,* SPCK, 1992.

Oxford University Press: *The Book of Common Worship of the Church of South India.* Used with permission.

Michael Perham (ed.): *Enriching the Christian Year,* SPCK/Alcuin Club, 1993.

The Right Reverend Kenneth Stevenson.

Westcott House, Cambridge.